LIVING FOR CRICKET

The Autobiography of Clive Lloyd

With a Foreword by Wes Hall

D1388491

LIVING FOR CRICKET

Clive Lloyd

With Tony Cozier

Foreword by Wes Hall

A STAR BOOK

published by
the Paperback Division of
W.H. ALLEN & Co. Ltd

A Star Book
Published in 1983
by the Paperback Division of
W.H. Allen & Co. Ltd
A Howard and Wyndham Company
44 Hill Street, London W1X 8LB

First published in Great Britain by
Stanley Paul & Co. Ltd 1980

Copyright © Clive Lloyd 1980, 1983

Printed in Great Britain by
Cox & Wyman Ltd, Reading

ISBN 0 352 31350 1

Contents

Acknowledgements

I should particularly like to thank Tony Cozier for all the help he has given me in the preparation of this book. He is, quite rightly, one of the most respected journalists in the world of cricket, and it was a pleasure working with him.

Special thanks are due also to Patrick Eagar, for most of the photographs are his, but also to the following photographers and agencies: *Daily Mirror*, G. Hallawell and P.B.L. Marketing.

Foreword by Wes Hall

I was flattered beyond words when Clive Lloyd asked me to write a few words as the foreword to his autobiography. Having reached the apex of his distinguished career as an outstanding cricketer and captain of the world's strongest Test team, Clive would have had a host of others on whom he could have readily called for such an assignment.

I have followed Clive's career with great interest ever since the day he made his debut, albeit belatedly, into Test cricket at the Brabourne Stadium in Bombay in 1966. I was a team-mate of his in his first three series and saw the power of his batting and the brilliance of his fielding at first hand. I also detected in those early days the signs of the respectability, strength of character and leadership qualities for which he will be remembered long after his exploits on the field are forgotten.

Not that the excitement which his batting and fielding have given to crowds the world over will be forgotten in a hurry. Who can forget a sizzling Lloyd drive through mid-off or pull over mid-wicket? Who can forget the many great innings he has played for Guyana, his adopted Lancashire and the West Indies? Who can forget his century in the first World Cup Final? Who can forget his cat-like figure pouncing on the ball at cover and firing it with pin-point accuracy back to the stumps for another run out? Who can forget a fielder I class alongside Colin Bland and Paul Sheahan as the finest in my time?

Yet, for me, it is Clive Lloyd the man and the captain who has made more of a mark on the sport he chose as his profession.

What are not often appreciated are the psychological problems which face West Indian cricket captains because of our varied religious, political and socio-economic back-grounds compounded by the insular tendencies of island peoples. In such circumstances, therefore, it is imperative that our captains are good leaders of men.

Like Frank Worrell before him, Clive Lloyd has proved to be such a man. Like Worrell, he has developed his players, built a team and achieved the feat of making it the strongest in the world. It is pertinent that so many of the stars of the present team started their Test careers under Lloyd – Richards, Greenidge, Roberts, Holding, Garner, Croft.

Clive has shown his strength of character by taking the highs and lows of his career with the same equanimity. There certainly have been several incidents to test his resilience – injuries, personal loss of form, defeat and, not least, the furore over the Packer affair.

In Australia in 1971, playing for the Rest of the World, he so badly injured his back in a fielding accident that he spent weeks in bed, semi-paralysed. It must have been an agonizing period, both physically and mentally, and yet he was back playing Test cricket within a couple of months. His recent knee injury in Australia kept him out of the team for the first Test and affected his form, yet he returned to score a century in the final Test.

In the West Indies, in 1973, the selectors dropped him from the team against Australia and left him so despondent that he considered quitting. I know. I was in the dressing room with him when, with tears in his eyes, I advised him to see it through. He did and, two Tests later, he was scoring 178.

The ignominy of the complete annihilation of his team by the Australians in 1975–6 hurt deeply and would have broken the spirit of a lesser man. But, within a few months, Clive was leading his team to a 3–0 victory over England in England.

A measure of the man can be seen from his position in what is known as the Packer affair. He resigned from the West Indies captaincy, a considerable sacrifice, on a matter of principle because he felt that West Indian cricketers, who are invariably from the proletariat, should be paid commensurately with their abilities.

He made his decision independently of the other players' views, and it is a measure of the esteem in which he is held by his players that they fully supported his stand.

There are no airs or graces about Clive Lloyd, no conceit nor self-importance. He is a likeable, soft-spoken individual, with a sense of humour, a strong devotion to his family and with all the qualities cricketers everywhere would do well to emulate.

In the long term, I would like to see the West Indian Cricket Board, in conjunction with Caribbean Community Governments, use his immeasurable talent and leadership qualities for the further development of the game. In the meantime, however, I would like to feel there are still plenty of runs left yet before he calls it a day.

1 The Early Days

Guyana is a large, sprawling country in South America, just a few degrees north of the equator and sandwiched in between Venezuela, Brazil and Surinam. As Guyanese are quick to point out, it is bigger by far than all the British Isles put together, but it is so under-populated that only 800,000 people inhabit its 83,000 square miles, most of them along the coastline of the Atlantic Ocean.

Only a few of the aboriginal Indians, the Amerindians, remain. Instead, the majority of the population consists of those of African and Indian descent, the former brought across the Atlantic as slaves, as they were to the rest of the hemisphere, in the seventeenth and eighteenth centuries; the latter, somewhat later in the nineteenth century, as indentured labour. Together, they comprise about 80 per cent of the Guyanese people. The other 20 per cent consists of those of British, Dutch and Portuguese stock and Chinese. The result is one of the most cosmopolitan countries you can imagine.

The people are not only of diverse races but also of diverse cultures and religions. There are Christians of every conceivable denomination, Hindus and Moslems. The influence of western culture is strong but a number of old African and, even more strongly, Indian customs and traditions remain.

There are, however, two factors which are common to all Guyanese – cricket and the English language, both bequeathed by the British who colonized the country from 1831 until 1966, when British Guiana became the fully independent nation of Guyana. No other country on the South American continent either plays cricket or speaks English. Perhaps if the Spanish had been the colonizers Guyanese might have been soccer-mad, like their Latin neighbours.

But cricket was the game which dominated sporting and, indeed, national life. Like other British colonies in the region, Guyana quickly proved its cricketing strength and has given the West Indies and the world outstanding players. Cricket is one field of endeavour in which Guyanese, in common with other West Indians, can prove their worth internationally, and the exploits of players and teams are followed with intense interest.

When a Test match is played at Bourda, in the capital of Georgetown, the queues start to form as early as 4 a.m. and the ground is filled to its capacity long before the first ball is bowled. When the Tests are overseas, radio sets are to be seen everywhere and it's easy to tell whether the West Indies are winning or losing. You have only to look at the expression on people's faces!

This was the world I was born into on 31 August 1944, as the second child and first son of Arthur Christopher and Sylvia Thelma Lloyd. Eventually, the family was to grow to six children – two boys and four girls, large enough but not particularly unusual in Guyanese society at the time.

Our home, as were so many in the capital, Georgetown, was a modest, wooden-frame building on Crown Street in the suburb of Queenstown. We were, I suppose, a middle-class family. My father was a chauffeur for a local doctor and my mother was Minister of Home Affairs – cleaning, cooking, sewing and looking after her brood. We were by no means well-to-do but we were not impoverished and memories of my childhood are generally happy ones. They concern mainly the joys of childhood typical of any healthy young boy, discovering life around me, making friends and playing games – or, to be more correct, playing the game of cricket.

If you take a drive through Georgetown now, you see boys of all ages involved in a game of cricket wherever there is space enough for it – and sometimes where there is hardly any space at all. In the early 1950s, if that drive had been through the Queenstown area, you might have noticed a somewhat gangling youth either wielding an oversized bat made of local wood left-handed or bowling right-handed and hoping to knock over the cardboard box which served as the wicket. That would have been the Lloyd boy!

My parents had no interest in sport. Certainly I never heard my father talk much about cricket or soccer or athletics nor relate tales of his own exploits, as fathers seem inclined to do. Mum was probably just too busy to have cared much. Yet, if I hadn't have been committed to cricket purely and simply because I was born in Guyana, there were several other factors to motivate my interest.

My first cousin was a young man 10 years older than I by the name of Lance Gibbs. His mother was my mother's sister, and both, as it happened, were born in Barbados so, I suppose, the cricket blood in our veins ran even stronger. It is one of the many reasons why I have such a soft spot for that small island which has yielded so many of our great cricketers.

By the time I was big enough to start playing with the other boys in the front yard, Lance was already into his teens and winning approving nods with his bowling from those who mattered. There were others, too, who were to make their names in the game who played in that yard. Or, I should say, in those two yards. One was not quite big enough to accommodate the pitch and the run-up as well. Luckily, the fence dividing ours from next door's was broken so we simply batted in one and bowled from the other. I should point out that I came along and found the fence broken and never asked how it got so.

Apart from Lance, Colin Wiltshire and Richard Hector were among the others who used to play and play and play while their mothers fumed at home over a carefully prepared lunch which got colder and colder. They both went on to play for Guyana. We all knew that Robert Christiani lived just up the road, although he was too old to take part any more at that level, the same Christiani that we had heard radio commentators talk about and we had read about playing for the West Indies in far-off lands.

It was not long before I was venturing up to the Demerara Cricket Club, the famous DCC, one of Georgetown's strongest club teams. Lance, Colin Wiltshire and Richard Hector played there, and it was automatic that it would become my club too. It has been, in fact, my club for as long as I can remember.

On Saturdays, when the club matches in the Case Cup inter-club competition were being played, I would be at the DCC grounds, not far from where we lived, helping in every way they would let me – running off for ice, helping with the teas, operating the scoreboard. And, all the time, watching the top players in action. Guyana players like Bruiser Thomas and Babsy Dyer. And, of course, Lance who bowled just as well in our yard as he did for DCC!

As I grew older, I also grew bolder and would take part in net practice sessions, fielding everything I could get my hands on and enjoying every moment of it. Naturally, I would enjoy it more when someone commented, 'Well fielded, son', or, 'Great stop', and that type of thing. It made me want to excel every time and, from then, I concentrated on my fielding.

There was also the opportunity to bowl in the nets and, even though a young boy in short pants still had to know his place and was not allowed to bat, the senior members would occasionally give you a knock on the outfield in front of the pavilion. It simply served as a further source of addiction to the game.

I have often wondered, looking back, how I managed to fit in any school work at all in those days. If I wasn't actually playing cricket, I was thinking about cricket or talking about cricket or reading about cricket. My academic achievements must have been hampered but it never ran me into trouble at school. Schooling started at St Ambrose Primary School from where I moved on to Fountain AME Public School which was just starting and which, most conveniently, was situated next door to the DCC (a street away from my home). I then finished at Chatham High.

Cricket was not the only outdoor sport in which I took an interest. While at Fountain, I also became very keen on track and field and found that I could outrun most of the boys in the school. Perhaps it was the long legs that did it and I was competing in almost everything that was on the programme – the 100 yards, the 220, the 440, the 880 and both the jumps. And all without blood transfusions or anabolic steroids – although I will admit to indulging in some weight-training!

Of course, athletics did bring the satisfaction of winning something tangible, and I carried home quite a few trophies, including one from the prestigious inter-schools sports championships. Cricket offered nothing like that. Its rewards were more abstract, such as the sweet feeling of a well-time drive or the delight of a brilliant catch. And, all the time, there was the goal of being a Test cricketer.

By the time I was 14, therefore, I was looking at the world through rose-coloured spectacles. Well, not exactly rose-coloured. My glasses were large, round and not particularly attractive but they were necessary and they certainly made me see better.

The incident which caused another addition to the four-eyed variety of the human race occurred when I was 12 years of age. Walking home from school, I noticed two younger boys engaged in a furious fight. Always the mediator, I stepped in to part them and got a knock in the right eye with a ruler for my troubles.

It was painful at the time but I took no real notice of it until my vision started to deteriorate. I found it difficult to see the blackboard in the classroom and had to move up to the front row. I had to squint to make out the score on the DCC scoreboard. Much more importantly, while batting I was being struck on the legs far too frequently for my liking and, in the inter-school in which I was playing, being out l.b.w. time and again. The umpire couldn't have been wrong every time.

So it was off to the optician. First, drops were recommended but when they proved ineffective, spectacles were ordered, becoming – for better or for worse – part of the Lloyd physiogue for ever more.

As I was saying, I hardly had a care in the world at the age of 14. I was captaining Chatham High in the Chin Cup inter-school competition and doing well, and I still had a few years of schooling left. Or so I thought. I was soon brought to earth with a bump for, in 1958, my father died, an event which shook the family in more ways than one.

He had been the bread-winner and he had earned just enough to keep us going. There were no savings to speak of; insurance was something novel in those days, and there was none of that. As the eldest son (in fact, my younger brother was living in England at the time), the responsibility for maintaining the family rested on my shoulders.

I had a scholarship at Chatham and had completed the basic school-leaving examination but surely would have advanced to the General Certificate of Education Ordinary level. Now circumstances dictated otherwise, and, aged 16, I moved into a job in the administrative section of the Georgetown Hospital. My starting salary was $78 (approximately £16) a month before tax, which, in those days, was not all that bad – but it certainly didn't keep the Lloyd household in the lap of luxury either.

Actually, even though we never let the situation get on top of us, we were in dire straits. Yet, I felt proud that I was able to provide for my mother and sisters. With my father gone, I accepted that was my responsibility and, as I moved subsequently into professional cricket and the pay improved, I was able to pay for my sisters' education, sending two of them to the United States where they still live.

Mum, I might add, was a Rock of Gibraltar through it all and, even though she travelled to visit us all at our homes in England and America when we grew up and left, she herself remains with my youngest sister in the same house in Georgetown.

Perhaps the additional sense of responsibility was also good for my cricket although that may be only an opinion expressed on hindsight. Certainly, responsibility did not hamper it and, at the age of 15, I made my debut for DCC, playing in the Wight Cup, or Division 2, competition. After only a single match there I was catapulted into the first team for a Case Cup match against the Georgetown Cricket Club at their home ground which happened to be Bourda, the Test ground.

This came about quite by chance for another left-handed bat by the name of Moore dropped out of the side at the last moment and Fred Wills, the DCC captain, insisted that I take his place. It is not difficult to imagine my feelings.

It was the moment every young West Indian waits for. Bourda had, for me, been my Mecca. Whenever there was a big match there, we would be given a half-day from school and we would rush to gain a vantage point in the trees which encircle the ground. We would choose the one overlooking the sightscreen, a magnificent view, and we tried to be as early as possible. Somehow, we could never beat one particular Indian lad whose name I never got to know but who seemed to sleep in that tree whenever cricket was on.

Just a year before, in the 1957/8 season, I had seen my first Test from that tree – and watched as Gary Sobers got two centuries against Pakistan in a match which the West Indies won. I had hoped to see Lance in action for that was his first series but, for some reason, he had been dropped for the

16

match. Nevertheless, the atmosphere was electric and the cricket really good.

Now I was appearing on that same field for the first time against players who had been gods to me – Norman Wight, Colin Heron, Lennie Thomas, George Camacho, all of whom had played for British Guiana.

A few things about that match stand out in my mind. The first was the big boots I was wearing. Previously, I had used only tennis shoes so the boots, provided along with the Everton Weekes and Len Hutton autograph bats of my youth by Lance, were rather uncomfortable. Perhaps they were the cause of a couple of dropped catches!

The second point was the way I got out. I had made 12, when Norman Wight decided to come around the wicket to me. I played for turn (after all, everybody always said how much he turned) and was done easily through the gate, bowled off the pad. I had only been in about twenty minutes and, experienced as he was, Wight had picked up a flaw immediately. Obviously Case Cup cricket was tough.

The third realization was that there there was going to be criticism. After that very first innings, a well-known local writer, Charles Chichester, wrote in his column in the Sunday newspaper that I would never make a top-class cricketer. Later, I heard that Robert Christiani had ventured much the same opinion. Perhaps it was because no DCC batsman had gone on to West Indian honours, even after doing well at local and regional level, and they thought I would be another example.

It was the sort of comment that niggled me and I was determined to prove them wrong.

By 1963, I was an established member of the DCC side and enjoyed an outstanding season. It was one of those years when everything seemed to hit the middle of the bat, and the result was a Case Cup record of over 900 runs in the eight matches and a call to trials for the British Guiana team which was to play in Barbados.

Being in the list of invitees, however, didn't guarantee a place in the actual teams – as I soon found out. Three trials went by and the name of C.H. Lloyd appeared in none of them, despite Lance's characteristic protests. I was understandably disappointed and even more so when rain washed

17

out the final match for which I was included. So, despite my big scores in the club competition, I was omitted from the team without getting a hit in the trials.

Everyone at DCC kept telling me it was only a matter of time; I would just have to wait. It was a question of making runs in the Case Cup, the standard of which was extremely high, and the rest would follow. In those days, before the doors of English county cricket were open to overseas players and before the heavy international schedules, our leading players would remain at home. It was not unusual for as many as four Test players, along with several other first-class players, to be in a single match on opposing teams. When the teams from Berbice county, eighty miles down the coast, came to town they brought with them Rohan Kanhai, Basil Butcher, Joe Solomon and Ivan Madray – not a bad combination!

So I had to stick it out – with a lot of encouragement from two men.

During those years, I became very attached to Fred Wills, the DCC captain, who, I imagine, became a father-figure to me. A brilliant man, he was an outstanding lawyer, later to become Guyana's Foreign Minister, and if he was not a great cricketer himself, he knew the game backwards. I would love just chatting with him and would even spend hours in the law courts listening to him in action, so to speak, so that it was hardly surprising that for some time I entertained thoughts of studying law.

Another who was always ready with sound, fatherly advice was Berkeley Gaskin, a DCC stalwart whose playing days were over by the time I came along but who was active in administration, both at local and regional level. Both he and Fred always seemed to have faith in my ability to make it to the top – so much so that I sometimes felt a little embarrassed by their optimism.

When I did eventually get into the British Guiana side, there was to be a long anxious time before I satisfied Fred and Berkeley – and, not least, myself – that their optimism was not misplaced.

2 Into the Big Time

After the phenomenal season of 1963, 1964 was bound to be something of an anti-climax. Yet I continued doing reasonably well for DCC and, if nothing else, I had managed to make a name for myself as a fielder. Fielding was an aspect of the game that I really enjoyed and, far from being hard work, practice was a joy.

When trials for the 1964 regional tournament were held, the name C.H. Lloyd appeared and, on the experience of the previous year, I entered them with some misgivings. In contrast to 1963, when we played only two matches in Barbados, there was now a full slate – one in Barbados and two at home against Jamaica and Trinidad. The Windward and Leeward Island, such a force in West Indies cricket these days, were still on the outside.

There had always been talk among some players that there were strange happenings in the trials and now I saw for myself. There were cases of unbelievable run outs, catches floored which babies could have taken, and the generous serving-up of half-volleys to certain players. Usually the senior men were involved and some of the younger players came to the inescapable conclusion that they were favouring those from their own club and giving them a little assistance to impress the selectors, while deliberately trying to block competitors.

Of course, it was completely fraudulent but most of those in the know realized that it went on. I only hope that this feature of trials is a relic of the past – although I have my doubts, human nature being what it is.

In any case, I did gain selection to the team at long last for one match in that tournament, against Jamaica at Bourda. I did nothing spectacular, scoring 12 before I swung the fast bowler Lester King, down long leg's throat. Yet there was the satisfaction of being on a winning team since British Guiana recorded a massive victory by an innings. The selectors, however, didn't hold to the old adage about sticking to winning teams. I was dropped for the final match against Trinidad. Just what could I do to earn a chance to prove myself?

The opportunities the following season were limited. The Australians were on tour so there was no inter-territorial cricket, which left the match against the visitors as the only first-class encounter. Naturally, a big score in that match would have been a tremendous boost but it was not to be. Not many people made runs in a low-scoring contest and, although given every chance by batting at number 4, while Kanhai and Solomon rested for the Test match, I went for 2 and 17.

A call to be the emergency fielder in the Test that followed boosted my spirits and I did actually get on to the field once. Not to field, mind you, but to carry a message from Frank Worrell, who was the manager, to Gary Sobers, the skipper, advising him to move Lance Gibbs from short leg since he was the key bowler and could not afford to have his fingers injured. Still, there was a generous response from the crowd when I ran on and, at least, I was on a Test ground in whites!

I was also made to feel part of it all in the dressing room and, since the West Indies won comfortably and Lance took six for 29 in Australia's second innings, it was a happy occasion.

By now, I had had two first-class matches and hadn't exactly taken the world by storm. My patience was wearing a little thin but I sensed that 1966 would be a crucial season. The West Indies Board had initiated a regular, annual tournament for the Shell Shield. With the Windward and Leewards included as a joint team, there would be four matches. In addition, they were to be followed by a tour of England and I told myself, as I am sure every other aspiring candidate did, that good performances in the Shield would buy a ticket on the plane to England. Well, anyhow, that was what I imagined.

For some reason, all of Guyana's matches were to be played away from home, necessitating the naming of a squad of fourteen, rather than eleven which would have been the case for a home match. Even the Doubting Thomases conceded that the name of Lloyd should have been on the list and I was duly named for what was to be my first venture outside the shores of Guyana. It was something of a relief to get away from playing at home where the pressures to succeed are always so great, and I really looked forward to it.

Although I wanted desperately to play, I realized I was no automatic choice since our middle order comprised Kanhai at number 3, Butcher at number 4 and Solomon at number 5, great Test players each, and I did no more than carry the drinks in the first match against Trinidad in Port-of-Spain.

When we moved on to Barbados, my chance came. A little left-handed opening batsman by the name of Roy Fredericks, who had made his first-class debut back in 1964 in the same match as I did, was left out; the order was shuffled about and Lance, the captain, and Berkeley Gaskin, the manager, announced at the hotel that I was in.

I have never been one to worry too much before a match, of whatever type. On Fred Wills's advice, I only start batting when I get to the middle and play what I get when I'm out there, not imagining all sorts of things the night before or in the pavilion. Yet, on that occasion, I don't mind admitting the butterflies fluttered a bit. Barbados, after all, was no ordinary side.

Led by Sobers, their attack was spearheaded by Charlie Griffith whose reputation for yorkers and bouncers at extreme pace was well known across the cricket world. Their team then contained ten players who had either represented the West Indies in Test cricket or were subsequently to do so. It was formidable opposition and, as it turned out, we were soundly beaten by an innings.

It was a significant match for me. In the first innings, I fell leg before for a duck to a ball from Sobers which cut in. I could almost feel the knives being dug in back home as I walked dejectedly back to the pavilion, and I was crest-fallen. An incident at the close of play, however, touched a delicate chord and changed my mood from one of depression to determination.

Berkeley must have praised me in conversation with Sobers before the game and, in the dressing room afterwards, Sobers went across to him. 'I see your boy didn't get any, then,' he said. Berkeley, never one lost for words, responded in a flash: 'It's not my boy but a boy that I like – and don't forget there's a second innings.' It was all probably just good-natured banter between good friends and surely wasn't meant for my ears.

Yet I overheard it all and resolved not to let Berkeley – or

21

myself – down in the second innings. This is the effect any criticism has had on me for as long as I've held a cricket bat, so it may not have been such a bad thing after all.

When my turn came to bat in that second innings, we were 86 for four, trailing by something ridiculous like 300 odd on the first innings after an unmerciful double-century from Sobers. Yet the pitch was still good and, not before time, I found my Case Cup touch in a first-class match. A century was passed and I eventually got 107 most pleasurable runs. Pleasurable for me but, as was obvious from the look on his face, even more pleasurable for Berkeley.

That innings took a load off my mind. There was no more concern as to whether my next failure would be my last, no more going in to bat with a point to prove. Everything could be approached with a far more positive outlook, and the result was immediately favourable.

We went on to Jamaica and there I got my highest score in any type of cricket, 194 against Jamaica at Sabina Park in Kingston in our final match of the season. I couldn't remember having made that many runs, even in the front-yard games in Queenstown!

By then, everyone had become a selector and was choosing his team for England. Form was assessed and, to most of my fellow players at least, it seemed a foregone conclusion that I would be in the list of seventeen. Some of those who had been there were even telling me what a great place England was and how much I would enjoy playing there. I saw no reason to doubt their confidence for, after all, it was based on performance.

It proved to be a naïve assumption. The West Indies selectors, over the years, had not exactly established a record of logic or credibility in their deliberations and this time they created an even greater stir than usual, more by who they omitted than who they included.

To my great anguish, I was out. So too was the Barbadian opening batsman, Robin Bynoe, who had enjoyed an excellent Shield and who had appeared as much a certainty as I was. To say that I was dumbfounded would be to put it mildly. I am not ashamed to say that I cried the night the news came through during our last game of the season against the Combined Islands in St Kitts. Basil Butcher was my room-mate and he tried to console me, as did Lance. But I would not be consoled. I just could not understand – until much later when the internal bartering and manipulations of the selectors at that time were revealed to me. The system of appointment was manifestly wrong, with each of the four major territories represented on the panel – Barbados, Guyana, Jamaica and Trinidad along with the captain and, in this case, also Frank Worrell. It was only natural to assume that each individual would be supporting candidates more on insular considerations than on merit and, as it turned out, this is what did happen.

The story was that since the Guyanese selector would not back Bynoe's inclusion, the Barbadian would not back mine. In addition, I understood that the Trinidadian representative abstained when it came to voting for me since he said he had missed the Trinidad match and had never seen me play. Thus two young batsmen with every right to be in the team were left behind because of petty squabbling among selectors.

Naturally, I have got over that little episode with the passing of time, but it never ceases to amaze me how selectors managed to produce teams that made any sense with the panel constituted as it was in those days.

The system has changed since, and not before time. Now the Board nominates three selectors, without any reference to insular considerations, who sit along with the captain to select the teams. Although the complaints from one territory or another persist and the charges of favouritism are still made, the fact that each territory no longer has representation by right has reduced suspicion. After all, justice must not only be done but must also be seen to be done.

For all the criticism of the 1966 team, it performed wonders in England, with Sobers in unbelievable form. I had to follow its progress listening to the ball-by-ball commentaries back home, which did nothing to improve my standing in the clerical section of the Georgetown Hospital. The next time the West Indies went overseas, however, there would be no need to sneak a radio into the office. I was determined to be there in person.

3   Test Cricket at Last

There was no first-class cricket between the end of the 1966 Shell Shield in March and the start of the West Indies tour to India and Sri Lanka late in the year. My place on that team would depend on what happened in England. As it turned out, Joe Solomon announced his retirement from international cricket following that tour, and a middle-order batting place became open. The name C.H. Lloyd, therefore, was among the several changes which the selectors made.

From the time I heard the announcement on the radio, I was on cloud nine – even after I found out that I would be forced to give up the job at the hospital. An application for leave without pay was turned down but there was no way I was going to reject this chance, and I duly quit.

Somehow, the idea of something happening which would prevent me going became almost an obsession. When the table-tennis player, Gordon Stephens, a close personal friend, left for a fortnight for the annual Caribbean championships in Trinidad, he lent me his motor-cycle, but I never rode it for fear that I would have an accident and injure myself. There were times when I felt a little apprehensive even about shaving. After all, I might cut my throat!

As it turned out, nothing happened and the trip to India, my first outside the Caribbean, proved a great experience. Firstly, and most importantly, I did well, playing in all three Tests and scoring more runs than anyone else on tour except Sobers. It virtually meant that my future as a professional cricketer was assured; had I been a failure, it would have taken quite a while to re-establish claims to a West Indian place.

On the question of professionalism, which has become so prevalent in recent years, it is interesting to note that my fee for that tour was £500, out of which I had to purchase a blazer, cap, crest, bats, gloves, shirts and trousers. In short, everything. Yet, to a young man whose previous highest pay packet had been just over $100 a month at the hospital, it seemed a pretty lucrative deal.

In any case, I am sure I would have gone for nothing. The money was simply a bonus, for all I wanted to do was to play cricket for the West Indies.

Not only was my career established during that series but also a lot of my philosophy on life and on cricket. It was an important period for an impressionable 22-year-old experiencing the outside world really for the first time.

Frankly, I was not prepared for the shock which India provided. Cricketers tend to talk cricket and little else, so that I learned nothing about the country itself in chatting with those who had been before. Reading about it did provide more background information, but India is a place which cannot be adequately described in words.

I was struck forcibly by several aspects. The vastness of India was staggering, even to a Guyanese who likes to boast to fellow West Indians about the size of our country. The hospitality of the people and their love of cricket and cricketers was also most impressive. I was overwhelmed by what I found, perhaps because West Indians tend to take their cricketers in a matter-of-fact way, whereas in India we were treated as VIPs. Naturally, I had seen nothing approaching the immense stadiums at which the Tests were played – nor the huge crowds which attended. The Brabourne Stadium in Bombay and Eden Gardens in Calcutta are colossal and make grounds in the West Indies like Bourda, Sabina Park and Kensington Oval lilliputian by comparison.

The huge gap in living standards between those at the top and those at the bottom was, of course, most obvious, perhaps even more so to international cricketers treated so royally. Poverty is a fact of life, I suppose, and a problem in West Indian countries as well. But I have never experienced such desperate poverty as in India and I came to realize that, no matter how badly off you think you may be, there is always someone somewhere who is even worse off. I have held this outlook ever since, not only on life generally but on cricket as well. Whenever I have gone through a bad patch, I have tried to remember that others far better than I am have been that way before, and have seen it through.

The food and the habits of Indian people were also different but we were, after all, in a different country on the other side of the globe with different values. It would have been silly to have expected conditions as they were at home

25

and, even though it meant being careful about what you ate and drank, the tour itself was not half as bad as I had heard it made out to be. Certainly, I managed to go through it without any health problems.

Unfortunately, this was not the case with David Holford. David had been the 'find' of the tour of England and started the Indian trip where he had left off there, enjoying an outstanding first Test with the bat and with leg-spin bowling. Then, after the first Test, he complained of feeling ill, and for some time, was treated for all sorts of ailments except the correct one. Luckily, an old Indian doctor practising in New Delhi saw him and diagnosed the real problem, literally before it was too late. He had an acute attack of pleurisy and he had to remain in hospital in New Delhi for almost three weeks, not to play again on the tour. When he did rejoin us he had lost a lot of weight after enduring a debilitating illness.

That tour was also disillusioning in many ways. The West Indies team was, to me, almost a sacred preserve. Those who managed to gain selection, I imagined, regarded their cricket with complete seriousness and observed a strict sense of self-discipline.

This image was quickly shattered. I was most disappointed with the attitude of many of the senior players who appeared to do as they pleased and who seemed content in the feeling that their individual ability would carry them through, as it had in their earlier years. Now, however, many of them were getting on and observers noted a decline in our standards, even though we did win the series of three Tests by a 2–0 margin.

Sobers, as captain, never got the type of support he deserved from his senior players. He is one of the nicest fellows I have met in cricket, but he needed to be stronger in his handling of individuals.

I was shocked too, by the way some members of our team abused the privileged position they were in. They were reluctant to accept the hospitality of the Indians, who often felt slighted as a result, and some of our players would be rough and sharp in refusing the pleas of autograph-hunters. Perhaps it was because I was young at the time, but I felt honoured that someone wanted to speak to me or wanted my autograph.

In later years, when I became captain, these were incidents which I remembered in trying to instil in my players the need for a sense of discipline and respect for others.

It is not always easy for a top international sportsman to keep his cool, granted, and there are times when he will have had his fill of signing autographs and receiving invitations. However, there are ways of handling these without being offensive. After all, if you have no respect for others, how can you expect others to have respect for you – or for the West Indies, for that matter, since all West Indian cricketers are ambassadors for their countries and, indeed, for their race? Almost the only contact people in India, Australia and New Zealand, for instance, have with West Indians is through our cricketers and it is through them that their impressions of us are formed. Fortunately, these impressions seem to have been favourable over the years, and I hope those who play for the West Indies in the future ensure they remain that way.

It was in India, as well, that I first got to know Frank Worrell, a man who had so much to do with the high esteem in which West Indian cricket is held. I had seen him around at various times in the West Indies but had had no real contact. He happened to be in Calcutta during the second Test as part of a lecture tour of the country, and there were a few issues on which I sought his advice. The first was a disciplinary matter over whether one of the players should be sent home for a serious misdemeanour. I was roused from a deep sleep at two in the morning and summoned to a meeting of all the team to discuss it. Later, I sought Frank's advice, which was freely and sensibly given; there was a vote among all members and the individual was allowed to stay after, I believe, a stiff reprimand. At the same time Frank told me not to be bitter about my omission from the earlier tour of England. I could have gone there, he said, and found it difficult in the strange conditions and it would have been a setback. Instead, the pitches in India were much more like those in the West Indies and my success was almost guaranteed.

Only a few days later, I was back to Frank again – along with a few of the others. The second Test at Eden Gardens

27

had been halted by a riot, stands had been burned and crowds had been in the streets chanting – what they were saying we didn't know because it was not in English but it did sound menacing. We understood that there had been some scandal involving the over-selling of tickets and the problem was that there were simply too many people in the ground.

We took shelter in the dressing room when it all started, and eventually, four or five of us managed to stuff ourselves into one of the little Morris cars so common in India, and we were driven back to the hotel by an official. Others got back in similar fashion and none of us were injured, although Charlie Griffith somehow ran all the way from ground to hotel through what must have been unfamiliar streets, a distance of almost three miles.

Well, there was plenty of discussion about whether the match – and, indeed, whether the tour – should continue. A lot of the senior players seemed fed up and wanted to call the whole thing off and go back home. Personally, all I wanted to do was to play cricket and I am sure that was the case of several of the younger members in the side. In the end, I think Frank's word carried a lot of weight. He said, simply and logically, that we in the West Indies were not exactly blameless in the matter of crowd disturbances at cricket matches; there were reasons for them which were unrelated to cricket and if we went home we would have to consider the position of future teams to the West Indies every time a match was stopped by the crowd.

Frank's theme all the way through was not to rush anything without carefully examining all the implications – a principle to which I have held ever since.

From the playing point of view, the series was most enjoyable. I was, as they say, 'being blooded' and I did not expect to force my way into a Test side with middle-order batting comprising Kanhai, Butcher, Nurse and Sobers – unless I was lucky. In two innings in the minor matches before the first Test at Bombay, I managed nothing outstanding, 39 and 15, and I was prepared to serve duties as emergency fielder for the first Test, when, quite out of the blue, Sobers came across after nets on the first morning of the match and announced, 'You're in, Clive.'

Seymour Nurse had injured his finger and had failed a

28

fitness test providing me with this unexpected chance. It was no more than a half-hour before the first ball was to be bowled so there was no time to think much about it. Whatever nerves I may have had were helped considerably by the fact that India's captain, the Nawab of Pataudi, won the toss and batted first. This meant that I could get into the match without too much pressure on me, particularly since fielding was the one area in which I was supremely confident. By the time I came to bat on the second day, therefore, I was into the match and the fact that it was a Test hardly made any difference. I just went out and batted.

When I got in, we were 82 for three replying to India's 296, and Chandrasekhar had taken all three – Bynoe, Kanhai and Butcher. We had heard a lot about Chandrasekhar, and the slight impediment of his right arm, which gives him a freakish action and makes the ball fizz off the pitch. No one seemed to know what he bowled and all they could tell us was to watch out.

It took some time for me to work him out for he really did mix things up. I began shakily and was put down early on at slip off his bowling, but after a while I decided to treat him purely as a googly bowler since I found that, even though he could deliver a leg break, it did not turn all that much. In addition, I decided to commit myself to the front foot a lot since he tended to skid through off the pitch.

After about three-quarters of an hour, the ball began to come cleanly off the middle of the bat more frequently and I began to feel more at ease. I swept Chandrasekhar frequently and found that his line would stray as he became tired. In addition, we were helped by the fact that there was no one of even medium pace in the Indian side; when you got settled there was nothing to break your rhythm. Durani and Nadkarni were orthodox left-arm spinners and Ven-kataragahavan a straight forward off-spinner, although all three were top class. Chandrasekhar, in fact, was the quickest of the lot and he surprised our openers more than once with bouncers!

Conrad Hunte was my partner in a century stand for the fourth wicket. By the time I had been caught behind off Chandrasekhar for 82, the foundation had been laid for our eventual total of 421 and a lead of over 100. It would be dishonest to pretend that I took that start to my Test career in my stride. To be truthful, it did much for my ego.

The Indians made a spirited fight-back in that Test, and we found ourselves having to get 192 in the second innings. On a wearing pitch, this was a little more difficult than it appeared on the surface. This time, Kanhai asked to go lower in the order than his usual number 3 which, I felt at the time, was a rather odd request. In fact, we were quickly in the toils and I was in at 51 for three (including nightwatchman, Lance Gibbs), all the wickets naturally due to Chandra. When he also had Hunte at 90, there was a buzz around the ground – we still had a long way to go.

Imagine my surprise, therefore, when Sobers came to the crease, called me over and said that we would take it easy for a while, wait for Chandra to tire, and then accelerate. He was anxious the match should be over by three o'clock, he said, since he had been given a hot tip for a race at the local track by his good friend Josh Gifford, one of the English jockeys in India for the winter.

There was never a thought in Sobers's mind about us even losing another wicket, far less losing outright. His only concern was the time we should finish it off. It was the confidence of this amazing individual which must have communicated itself to me for we then played exactly as Sobers had indicated. We kept out Chandra for a while and, as the loose balls became more frequent, we started to find the gaps in the field and the boundaries with more regularity. In the end, I was 78 not out, Gary 53 not out, and he did get to the race track to find out how Josh Gifford's tip made out.

Unfortunately, I can't complete the story properly since I never did remember to ask him whether his horse won or lost. My concern was more for the win we had achieved in the Test, pleased with the part I played in it.

That match marked my first encounter with Chandra-sekhar and Venkataragahavan. In the very next one, against a Prime Minister's XI at New Delhi, a match in which I got my first century in West Indian colours, we came across the two other spinners of the quartet which served India so magnificently in the following decade, and whose names were altogether more pronounceable than the other two – Bishen Bedi and Erapalli Prasanna; to us, they were Bish,

Chandra, Pras and Venkat. They were to pose problems for West Indian batsmen several times thereafter.

The Calcutta Test, despite the riot, provided an innings victory for the West Indies, principally on the spin of the coin. We batted when the pitch was at its best, got 390 and, the pitch became more and more broken up, India failed to pass 200 in either innings. It must have assisted spin because my far-from-venomous leg-spin accounted for the illustrious wickets of Chandu Borde and Pataudi in the second innings, some compensation for failing with the bat.

At that stage, two up with one to go, a noticeable air of complacency swept through the team and we were fortunate not to lose the last Test outright after we had been completely outbatted by the Indians. In fact, everyone had written the match off as lost when our seventh wicket fell in the second innings and Griffith joined Sobers with something like two hours to go. Somehow they held out, the miraculous Sobers completing yet another Houdini act for the West Indies and Griffith, using pads, body and, once, even his neck, to obstruct the ball, remaining with him as the Indians were kept at bay.

This partnership managed to keep our unbeaten record against India intact, but you couldn't help but feel that a golden era in West Indian cricket was coming to a close as some of the great players were nearing the end of their days. As far as I was concerned, however, my cricketing days were just beginning.

4   The Lancashire Connection

I had never heard of Haslingden or knew such a town existed until Wes Hall mentioned to me in India that a club of that name played cricket in the Lancashire League and needed someone to replace Clairmonte dePeiza as professional. Would I be interested?

The answer was obvious. Several of the great West Indian cricketers had played in the English Leagues, and I had heard some of those in the team in India discussing their experiences. Wes advised strongly that I go, and so did Lance and Frank Worrell when they heard about the offer. I needed no persuasion; it meant that I would be playing cricket full time and being paid for it.

After making contact with Tom Lees, the Haslingden secretary, the deal was settled. I briefly went back to the West Indies from India, and then said farewell yet again to my mother and friends to start out on what was possibly the most fateful journey of my life. I did not know it at the time but I was travelling to a part of the world, Lancashire, which was to become my adopted and beloved home.

Apart from the skimpy second-hand reports from fellow cricketers – whose stories you can always take with a pinch of salt anyway – I had no idea what to expect at Haslingden and a feeling of apprehension was only natural. I need not have worried.

The people of the town, some eighteen miles outside Manchester, could not have been warmer or more welcoming. Everyone seemed so glad to have me playing for them and, as I enjoyed an excellent first season, they were still happier, even though the team did nothing remarkable. They would boast about the exploits of 'their' professional and talk about the six that he hit into the adjoining building or the catch that he took.

I was flattered, and it stimulated me to do as well as I possibly could. Perhaps that inspiration helped me to score 861 runs, which was the highest in the League, and to take 47 wickets.

Whether it was in the club bar after the game over a pint or two of the local bitter (to which I took some time to become

accustomed), on the streets and at the small hotel, the
Woolpack, run by the family Cook, where I stayed, I was
made to feel completely at home. Happily, Haslingden's
President, John Entwistle, appeared to take an immediate
liking to me and, in turn, me to him and we got on
wonderfully. Long after I had left Haslingden, I continued to
see him regularly and we are firm friends to this day.

Haslingden had hired West Indian pros long before I came
along and obviously they had made an excellent impression,
helping to pave the way for my reception. The great George
Headley had been with them in the 1930s, and J.K. Holt and
dePeiza in more recent years.

Cricket in the Leagues was like nothing else I had
encountered before. One innings matches were played
between teams from towns in the area every Saturday and
some Sundays – that is when the rain allowed it. Each team
had its professional who was expected to carry the side,
bowling, batting and fielding. This was not to say that the ten
amateurs who made up the eleven were merely there to fill in
numbers, and there were a few very good players around
who might well have gone on to county standard had they
had opportunity or inclination.

Yet it was only natural that the professional, always
someone with Test or first-class experience, was the Big
Chief. He was the one the spectators came to see and, if he
did well, he could expect a collection around the ground in
appreciation of the particular performance. My first was not
long in coming as I got a century against Enfield in my very
first match only to discover that, by custom, the takings
went into buying drinks all round at the club bar!

The notion that the Leagues were for has-beens and never-
wases was also false. The first year I played at Haslingden
there were men like Neil Hawke, Frank Misson, Charlie
Griffith, Ikram Elahi and Chester Watson with other clubs –
and all playing their hearts out just as I was doing as
Haslingden.

It is said that playing cricket in England improves your
game by tightening batting technique. That may have been
correct as I did detect an improvement in my batting style as
a result of one season with Haslingden. What I did recognize
more forcibly, however, was that I concentrated more,

undoubtedly because I was in a team which depended so heavily on my contribution. Knowing that failure would put an enormous burden on the others, I buckled down and became more responsible as a result.

If I had listened to the good-natured complaints of the Haslingden groundsman, I might also have curbed the inclination I have always had to lift the ball out of the ground. It was not a particularly big ground, with an auction barn on one side, and quite a few balls were lost from my bat in that direction. 'You know, you're costing this club a hell of a lot of money,' the groundsman used to quip every time the ball failed to return from one of my six-hits.

It was at Haslingden, too, that I started to bowl medium-pace seam-up, the standard operating procedure, it seemed, in England. In that first season, there was hardly a day in May when it did not rain, and we would squelch on to the field with water up to our boots and have to bowl on soft puddings as pitches. Leg-spin certainly made no sense in those conditions.

While at Haslingden I made my initial contact with Lancashire Cricket Club. It was automatic that during the extraordinarily wet period early in the 1967 season I would find my way into the indoor nets at Old Trafford along with some of the other pros in the League; in this way we kept in touch. A few of the Lancashire lads – Barry Wood I distinctly remember – would be in attendance and, I'm presumptuous enough to believe, took some mental notes.

This was the period in which the doors of county cricket were being thrown open to overseas players and there was a keenness on both sides, counties and cricketers, to take advantage of the new regulations. Already playing were such as Roy Marshall, Hampshires long-standing Barbadian, Keith Boyce at Essex, John Shepherd at Kent, and Lance Gibbs at Warwickshire, but these had all had to fulfil their residential qualification period. Now qualification would be instant.

In addition to my cricket with Haslingden, I played a lot for Derrick Robins's XI in the week during that 1967 season and must have done enough to convince the powers that be at Old Trafford that I was a worthy enough candidate for their Lancashire team. Before the summer was out, Jack

Wood, the secretary, had sounded me out about the possibility of joining the county.

Their other choice, although I was unaware of it then, was Farokh Engineer, the Indian wicketkeeper–batsman who was touring England at the time and with whom I had become quite friendly after attending his engagement party in Bombay the previous winter during our tour there. Both of us subsequently did join to become very much part of the Lancashire cricket scene, spending many happy hours together both on and off the field.

My decision, however, was not immediate. It had been hinted during those Robins games that Warwickshire would also be interested. In any case, I still had a year of my Haslingden contract to go, and there was no possibility of letting them down. In addition, even though everyone was convinced that the way would be cleared for the overseas players to come in, the MCC was still humming and hawing about the exact formula to be used and I was not going into something until I knew precisely what it was going to entail.

So I went back to the Caribbean in October to prepare for the 1967/8 series against England still undecided about the matter. It was at the Queen's Park Oval, at Port-of-Spain, during the first Test that it was finally resolved. I was put on the spot by a cable with a definite offer from Lancashire and did not take very long to reply in the affirmative. I knew the area and the people well and that was a crucial consideration.

Whether it would have been that way had Lance Gibbs put forward the offer which he was apparently commissioned to do on Warwickshire's behalf is difficult to say. Certainly his influence would have had great bearing on my final choice, and possibly also the fact that they were supposedly prepared to pay almost double the £2500 I was to receive from Lancashire. For some reason, however, he never broached the subject until the cable arrived from Old Trafford and then he made no effort to advance his own county's claims.

By the time I returned to England in the spring of 1968, then, it was known that it was to be my last season at Haslingden before moving on to Lancashire. Perhaps it was not the best time to ask for a rise but I did; I felt it was justified after my performances in the previous season and the fact that I had done well against England in the series in the West Indies which had been so fully reported in England.

However, the committee baulked and gave a flat rejection. There was no ill feeling or anything like that but John Entwistle stepped in, told me he personally thought I deserved more and paid the extra himself. It was a truly magnanimous gesture and I was happy that I could reward him with another productive season – this time 1226 runs at an average of over 56 an innings, which was almost 300 runs better than the Australian, Ian Brayshaw, who had the second highest aggregate. Unfortunately, the club could do no better than finish middle of the table.

In that second season, I moved into a flat with an old friend, Keith Barker, a Barbadian all-rounder who had been professional with the Georgetown Cricket Club and who was now playing with Walsden in the Central Lancashire League. It was situated at Clayton-le-Moors and, once more, the warmth of the Lancastrian people – if not the Lancastrian climate – was something to be marvelled at.

It was some time after I had signed with them before I could enjoy a full season with Lancashire. In 1968, I had only a few matches for the seconds and then, in 1969, I was with the West Indies touring party during the first half of the summer which limited me to fewer than a dozen games.

The fact that I had signed, of course, did cause much comment. Most was favourable and it appeared that Old Trafford would be as happy to have me as Haslingden had been. Yet there were one or two queries and I understood that one player even resigned because he felt I had come in as an outsider and would be getting more than he was. If the dressing room was a little bit cold at first, I put this down either to the weather or the normal period before any new player gets to feel at home in any team. Yet, that initial apprehension didn't last long, for you don't share your life with twelve or thirteen other individuals day in and day out without getting to feel almost as part of a family. Perhaps there comes a time when the county player can become fed up with seeing too much of the same faces, the same grounds, the same motorways, the same hotels – particularly when his team is doing poorly and the weather is rotten.

It is then that the captain's mettle is demonstrated, and I was lucky that I came in when Jackie Bond was at the helm. Jackie was, in a word, magnificent. He had given his all to Lancashire over the years and was appointed, to widespread surprise, as captain in 1968 at the age of 36 when the county's fortunes were at a low ebb. He could hardly be described as a great player, an efficient middle-order batsman who had never quite secured his place in the Lancashire first team, nor a brilliant tactician. Yet he had the quality of leadership. His own enthusiasm and dedication proved infectious. He understood his fellow players and they understood him and, until he retired from the game in 1973, I do not believe it was possible to find a more popular captain anywhere.

My first season at Old Trafford coincided with his appointment. When I played my first championship match, against Gloucestershire at Bristol, I had left the West Indies at Southampton the day before having got 80-odd against Hampshire. So I was in pretty good form and determined to make my debut appearance for the county one to remember. The result: 0 in the first innings and 2 in the second.

Jackie clearly realized my disappointment as I must have been sitting in the corner of the dressing room, looking rather sorry for myself. He came across, put his hands on my shoulder and said: 'Look, Clive, you don't have to prove yourself to us or anyone else. We know you're a fine player and you've got the record to prove it. You'll come good soon.' Not particularly inspiring stuff on the face of it, perhaps, but I can never forget how much it meant to me at the time – the right words at the right time, if you like.

And, of course, things did 'come good', not only for myself but for Lancashire as well. The John Player Sunday League started in 1969 and we won that. In 1970, we retained the JPL title and added the Gillette Cup as well, the first of a hat-trick of victories in the premier limited-overs competition.

We became the 'one-day kings' of English cricket. The interest in our matches was phenomenal and we would regularly have Old Trafford packed to capacity on Sundays and for the Gillette matches. We started to attract new followers while the old, established membership delighted in our success – although I suspected that not everyone was too enraptured by the influence of the various limited-overs competitions.

The players, however, were having a grand time. To hear thousands of Lancastrian voices raised in song supporting their team was something previously heard only across the road at United's Old Trafford, and it certainly gave us all a tremendous boost. I don't think anyone will ever forget the day in 1970 when 33,000 came to watch us win our final match and so take the John Player title. That the opposition was Yorkshire made it all the sweeter. The spirit, as is not difficult to imagine, was remarkable and we had a well-balanced, well-led team.

It was hard to better the 1970 side, which beat Sussex in the Gillette Final, as a county combination, no matter what type of competition was being played. It was, in batting order, Barry Wood, David Lloyd, Harry Pilling, yours truly, John Sullivan, Rookie Engineer, Jackie Bond, David Hughes, Jack Simmons, Ken Shuttleworth and Peter Lever. In that eleven, there was batting down to number 9 and bowling of every type – Shuttleworth and Lever fast; Woodie and myself as medium-pacers (no funny comments, please!); David Hughes left-arm spin and 'Flat Jack' Simmons, the meanest 'off-spin' bowler around.

In addition, we were, without boasting in any way, the best fielding team around. The two Lloyds seemed to want to outdo each other, young Frank Hayes was as fast as lightning and every catch seemed to stick. In addition, Engineer was a real jack-in-the-box behind the stumps and he helped make it all look good. The truth was that we enjoyed our cricket and the crowds seemed to enjoy us – not only at home for we generally attracted big gates away as well.

What I found most stimulating, from my own point of view, was the way I was treated and accepted by our followers. To them, I was not an 'overseas player' or an outsider. Whether it was chatting around the bar after the game or in a casual meeting with someone while signing an autograph or from the many letters which I received, it was clear that, to everyone in Lancashire, I was a Lancastrian through and through, and that meant a lot to me.

This was the Haslingden spirit all over again, and I even

found myself caught up in the traditional fervour of the Roses battle against Yorkshire, even if I couldn't quite master the northern accent.

I had heard about the rivalry with Yorkshire long before coming to Manchester but to experience it on the cricket field was tremendous. I don't think our record against them is particularly flattering but I've somehow always got runs against them, probably because the old adrenalin is pumping almost as if it were a Test. Even though we lost, I particularly enjoyed our game against them at Leeds last summer (1979). We had to fight back from a first-innings deficit of something like 160 and yet we carried them down to the final over. The fact that I got 103 in the second innings might just have added to the enjoyment!

If I make Lancashire sound something like a cricketing Utopia, all I can say is that it was. Those were some of the happiest days of my career, and the one tiff with the authorities which angered me was only minor. During my first season, I found it difficult to find proper accommodation and moved from place to place, a most unsatisfactory arrangement. So I complained to Jackie Bond and said that if the county could not find me something permanent and decent, I would have to think over my future with them. As usual, Jackie saw reason and, in no time, I had my own flat in Didsbury which I shared with Winston English, the Guyanese professional who replaced me at Haslingden, until a rather attractive young nurse ended my days of bachelorhood in 1971 and we moved into our own home in Peel Hall.

Naturally, Lancashire were not going to rule English cricket for ever and, inevitably, there came a time when we began to struggle. Other teams became stronger and found the formula for the one-day game while we gradually began to lose our zest. Many of our key players became older and found the pace more and more demanding. Jackie Bond's days came to an end, and the captaincy was given to David Lloyd who took over at a difficult period. No matter who succeeded him, the new captain wouldn't fill Jackie's boots perfectly, and problems of injury and loss of form of key players, along with Test calls at vital times, compounded the issue.

When David was appointed, I will admit that I was aggrieved for I had hoped for the job myself. I felt that the players wanted me, something which was confirmed to me by no less a person than the secretary, Jack Wood, who revealed that I had received overwhelming support in a straw poll taken among them. So why was I passed over and made vice-captain instead? Was there some racial consideration, or was it just that the committee felt they wanted a Lancastrian in the post? I hoped it was the latter.

In fact, there were several times in 1974, while David was on Test duty against India and Pakistan, when I did lead Lancashire, enjoying it immensely and taking the opportunity to put in some match-practice, as it were, since I had just been appointed West Indies Captain for the 1974–5 tour to India, Sri Lanka and Pakistan.

The Lancashire captaincy was again open when David decided to resign after the county had two disastrous years in 1976 and 1977 and, like all skippers, he had taken the brunt of the blame. By then, however, the storm over the Packer business had broken with all its fury, I had operations for the removal of both cartilages which restricted my appearances, and there was the feeling abroad that counties should be led by those with the potential to lead England which, after all, is fair enough.

I deal in some detail somewhat later with the Packer affair which so shook the cricket world in 1977 and my comments here are confined to its effect on my standing in Lancashire. Personally very few of us who signed for World Series Cricket realized what emotions it would arouse and how completely we would be ostracized for it. Certainly I had no idea until I found certain members at Old Trafford noticeably shunning me, and I detected a distinct coldness instead of the usual northern warmth which had always been forthcoming in the past.

Of course, not everyone took that attitude, and there was no noticeable change in the players. Yet it only made things tougher for those tireless workers who organized my benefit – particularly since the year also happened to coincide with the operations which kept me down to three innings all season. In spite of everything, those on the committee worked like Trojans on my behalf and, in the end, my benefit realized nearly £30,000.

As far as I was concerned, I could not see why my contract with Packer should in any way affect my relations with Lancashire. There was absolutely no conflict between the Australian and English seasons and, if there had been, I would have been forced to think long and hard before making a decision to leave Lancashire – no matter what the World Series Cricket fee. Over the years, Lancashire has become my home and my county and I feel committed to its cricket and its cricketers.

Just recently, we have floundered a bit at Old Trafford and, for some reason, the young players who appeared to have so much potential early on have not developed as we had hoped. However, as Jackie Bond would say, 'things will come good' again – and, I am sure, sooner rather than later. I hope to be around when they do, for Lancashire cricket is dear to my heart and always will be.

5 In the Doldrums, West Indies ...

If the West Indies victories in two of the three Tests in India in 1966-7 were enough to camouflage the beginning of the end of a great era in West Indies cricket, the decline against England at home in 1968 and then on tour to Australia and New Zealand in 1968-9 could not be hidden.

Many of the leading players were coming to the end of their days and a general lack of dedication was clear during my first tour to India. These became even more glaringly evident through the next two series.

In retrospect, we needed to include more young players, particularly fast bowlers, to groom them for the immediate future. Wes Hall and Charlie Griffith, probably the greatest combination of fast bowlers the West Indies has produced, had written their names in the history books through their magnificent contributions to the golden era of the early 1960s. Now, however, their fitness was in doubt, and they found it difficult to get through matches without being handicapped by injury.

I felt someone like Vanburn Holder, young, strong and fast, could have been tried. He had played in the Shield in 1967, and Tom Graveney quickly noticed his potential during the 1968 MCC tour of the Caribbean and signed him up for what was to be a long and distinguished career for Worcestershire. Lester King, the bustling Jamaican, was another who could have filled the bill.

As it was, Wes and Griff went on a bit too long and, instead of ending their careers in justifiable glory, went out in disappointing anti-climax.

Personally, I had nothing to complain about since my place in the team was settled and I continued to get runs. Yet it is important to be in a winning and happy side and it was a long time before any West Indian team could be so described again.

The 1968 series against England is a fine example of the point I am making. My own performance was most satisfying. My first Test innings on West Indian soil brought me a century, 118 to be exact. Ironically, it was at the Queen's Park Oval which, subsequently, has become something of a bogey ground for me. In those days, the pitch was a real beauty, hard and true with an even bounce; now it is so unpredictable and slow.

I got another century in the third Test at Kensington Oval where, of course, I had scored my debut Shield hundred two years earlier and where I have always felt competely at ease. The pitch there was good then, is good now and, I believe, will always be good. With its large sightscreens, clear light and knowledgeable crowd, Kensington would rank very high on my list of priorities when Judgement Day comes and I am given a choice of grounds to play on for eternity!

An average of over 50 against an England attack of John Snow, David Brown, Jeff Jones, Fred Titmus, Pat Pocock, Tony Lock and Basil D'Oliveira would have pleased any 23-year-old in only his second series, and I don't mind admitting that I was happy with my form. It is always more gratifying when you play well with the team up against it, and the first Test century was made in such a situation. We were 124 for three replying to England's huge 568 and it was to be one of those days for me. I had not faced any of the England bowlers before, but soon worked out that Fred Titmus was not a true off-spinner as such but rather a 'drifter', bowling slow in-swingers to the left-hand. So I swept him. I had an early six and almost before I knew it, I had passed the magic hundred mark. Even so, we had to follow on and just managed to save the game with Sobers and Hall batting out the final session.

My memories of that series, however, were not of my own performances but of three quite remarkable Test matches.

One was the second, at Kingston's Sabina Park, which was played on the worst pitch I have encountered in Test cricket. The pitch there is normally cracked, but appearances are generally deceptive and, over the years, it has been an excellent wicket, fast and true. On this occasion, however, it had recently been relaid and there it wasn't so much cracks that criss-crossed the surface but rather gaping crevasses. It looked like the Grand Canyon and Tom Graveney swore he got an echo back when he shouted into one crack.

England's first innings of 376 was made before things started to happen. By the time we went in, however, there was simply no telling what the ball would do once it pitched.

Snow, Brown and Jones made life a misery. We were quickly out for 143 and, for the second Test in succession, followed on. Snow took seven wickets and, although I somehow managed to top-score with an undefeated 34, it was a painful experience as Jones, left-arm over the wicket, consistently hit the fleshy, unprotected parts of the body with deliveries that leapt viciously out of the cracks.

In our second innings, there were two masterful innings by Nurse and Sobers who played shots that were magnificent in any conditions but double the value in these.

And there was also bottle-throwing by the crowd. We were 204 and still behind when Butcher was fifth out caught down the leg-side by the keeper, always an annoying way to go. As he walked off, Butch slapped his pad with the bat, a gesture of annoyance with himself. However, the crowd apparently took it as a sign of disagreement with the umpire and, in no time, bottles and stones were being hurled around. The riot squad came and, ignoring the direction of the strong wind, tossed teargas canisters into the section of the ground where the trouble had started. Since the breeze was blowing in the opposite direction, those who got the nauseating effect of the teargas were not the bottle-throwers at all but those of us in the pavilion on the western side!

There were several tearful eyes among the players as we returned to our hotel that night, leaving officials to determine what to do about the seventy-five minutes lost because of the disturbance. I could not help but recall the attitude of Sir Frank Worrell during similar circumstances in Calcutta only a year before and appreciate again his calmness in that situation. He had died in the interim, a sad and unexpected loss to us all, and I think many of those who had then been keen to return home from India now saw the wisdom of Sir Frank's advice.

As it was, England requested that the lost time be added on the unscheduled sixth day, which was not unreasonable since they appeared to be in a winning position at the time. Yet, thanks to Sobers's phenomenal 113 not out and support from the lower order, we actually declared with nine wickets down, a typical piece of Sobers bravado, and set about trying to win the match. We almost did and when time was called on that additional sixth morning, before we all scrambled out to the airport to catch our flight south, England were 68 for eight. The ball did frightening things on that final day, and poor Jim Parks was hit flush on the Adam's Apple by a delivery from Hall which leapt at him from one of the gigantic cracks on the pitch.

The next surprise package occurred in the final day of the fourth Test at Port-of-Spain in which, for the first time, we had had the better of exchanges. Yet, it was such a high-scoring match and England batted so safely after we had scored well over 500 that the first definite result of the series was out of the question, certainly as far as I was concerned. This assumption, I am sure, was held by most people, including several members of the West Indies team.

Suddenly, just after lunch, Sobers clapped from the pavilion and summoned his batsmen off the field. He had declared, setting England 215 to win in the remaining two and three-quarter hours' play. Our declaration came as such a bolt out of the blue that I was simply not prepared for it. Someone in the dressing room did mention that it takes only ten balls to take ten wickets, and there were references to Basil Butcher's spell in the first innings when he got five quick wickets, and the greyish look of the pitch was mentioned. Yet, to this day, I cannot understand how we were expected to bowl out a team including Edrich, Boycott, Cowdrey, Barrington, Graveney and D'Oliveira in a half-day – with an attack from which Griffith was missing through injury and which was opened by Sobers and Gibbs, of all people.

Of course, we didn't and England, with a masterful display from Boycott and Cowdrey, won by seven wickets with a few minutes to spare to the utter consternation of all West Indians. Perhaps consternation is too mild a word. Disgust, shock, disbelief would be more appropriate. Personally, I just sat in the corner of the dressing room, disconsolate, and wept, I was so emotionally keyed up. It was the first time I had been in a losing West Indian team and the effect of the defeat – and its method – staggered me. The faces of others in that dressing room told the same story.

If the players were crestfallen, the public was even more so. There was an eerie silence when we walked out of the ground through normally noisy spectators and when we went from Port-of-Spain to Georgetown for the final Test next day, immigration and customs officials at the airports, always so anxious to chat about the game, seemed embarrassed to raise the subject. There's the story that one customs man asked Gary if he had anything to declare, to which the skipper replied: 'Never again!' But I'd take that with a pinch of salt!

Poor Gary. He came under tremendous pressure. They hung an effigy of him in Independence Square in Port-of-Spain and he was criticized everywhere. And that was Sobers, the God, mind you. It was then that I really came to realize what losing meant to West Indians – a lesson I have never forgotten.

Another lesson to be learnt in the final Test at Georgetown also had to do with losing. We knew we had to win that one to square the rubber. Gary played his heart out, almost as if he personally wanted to atone for his decision to declare in Trinidad. He scored 152 and 95 not out, bowled 68 overs in the match and took three wickets in each innings. England were left with the last day of the series to bat to protect their one-game advantage; when they were 41 for five, we seemed almost home with Lance Gibbs well on top and bowling beautifully.

However, Cowdrey and Knott fought back, and full credit to them for a partnership of 127 which held us at bay. Throughout England's second innings, however, there were blatant time-wasting tactics. Cowdrey actually ran into the pavilion to change a pad, taking up five valuable minutes. He called for a glass of water to be brought on to the field and, at one stage, waited until crowd noise subsided, accounting for more valuable time. And to think that he had gained the captaincy after Brian Close had been sacked for time-wasting in a county match the previous summer!

Well, we just failed to pull that one off, Jeff Jones, the number 11, surviving the final over of the match from Gibbs amidst enervating tension to clinch the draw England needed to regain the Wisden Trophy.

It was throughout that series, too, that I realized that most Test players were not inclined to *walk* even though it was clear they were out. Kanhai did in the first Test when Cowdrey caught him low down at slip and indicated that he had taken the ball cleanly, but there was none of it from the other side. Until then, I had always been under the mistaken impression that cricket was a 'gentleman's game' and that *walking* was part of its great tradition. However, when I watched players who had been gods to me in my youth stand there and await an umpire's verdict when they had hit the ball hard, my mind and my attitude changed.

So after five consecutive victorious series, the West Indies had tasted defeat. This should have been the time to take stock and to act accordingly for the strenuous tour of Australia and New Zealand which followed at the end of the year. Unfortunately, the selectors showed no such foresight when they announced the names of the seventeen players for that trip immediately after the fifth Test in Georgetown. Of those who played in the series, only Deryck Murray was omitted – a strange decision since he had played in all five Tests and was only 27 years of age at the time.

We went to Australia and New Zealand, for five and a half months of some of the hardest cricket possible, with the majority of players on the wrong side of 30, many of them knowing this was their last tour with the West Indies. They were not as fit as they used to be, not as keen, not as dedicated, and, in many cases, not as good.

It was a formula for disaster, particularly since the team lacked the firm leadership so necessary in such situations. Sobers had never been a disciplinarian. It was not in his nature. He had come up through the ranks with the majority of those now under him; they had formed a winning combination on their sheer cricketing talent and the fact that they were so well balanced. Sobers expected every player to impose his own self-discipline. They were all 'big men', he would say, capable of looking after themselves. His philosophy might have been all right a few years earlier but it was out of place now. Perhaps it was in the manager's jurisdiction to enforce the type of regimentation needed to achieve results on the field but Berkeley Gaskin was now in his sixties and he was not strong enough.

Very little went right on that tour but we had ourselves to blame, firstly for team selection and secondly for the absence of discipline and direction. Hall and Griffith were again chosen which, I thought, was unfair to them both. Neither was fit enough and, although they bowled well at intervals, they were never able to provide the sustained effort which was needed and which someone like Vanburn Holder might have been able to give.

In addition, no thought was given to training schedules, net sessions and team meetings. We dropped so many catches that you needed a calculator to tot them up. I believe, in the end, it worked out to something like thirty-six in the five Tests. Yet we very rarely had any catching practice – an hour or so which would have sharpened up reflexes dulled by the passing years. Neither did I see anyone going on training runs and several players became overweight. Team meetings were a shambles; there was no proper discussion about how we should bowl to batsmen like Bill Lawry, Ian Chappell and Doug Walters who were making piles of runs off us. It was interesting to me when, later, the Englishmen kept removing Walters to gully catches.

There were mumblings in the camp that Sobers was batting too low and should promote himself above the number 6 position which he now seemed to favour. Most people felt he was leaving himself exposed to the likelihood of running out of partners. Well, it was some time before the suggestion was formally made at a team meeting by yours truly. Gary thought about it, said he would give it a try and then never did until the fourth Test when, incidentally, he failed. The idea was then put out of mind.

Gary himself got most of the blame for the débâcle and the 3–1 thrashing which we eventually suffered. It is traditional that the skipper gets the stick for his team's poor performance, the same as a prime minister does for a government, and in many ways criticism was justified. Gary did spend a lot of time on the golf course and not enough in the nets, looking after his team. However, I personally believe some of his problems with the team should have been handled by the manager.

Yet it was nothing new and, rightly or wrongly, Gary felt he was being unfairly treated by the press. Perhaps he found it difficult to accept that the great team in which he had played such a leading part in the early 1960s was now dissipating.

One additional millstone around our necks, I felt, was the

48

preceding 1960-1 tour under Frank Worrell, which had been such a rousing success with its tied Test and remarkable sequence of close finishes and thrilling cricket. Australians appeared to expect a repeat performance when everyone knew full well that was impossible.

As far as the Australian team was concerned, they had one aim, as always – to beat the living daylights out of us. Lawry was now captain and he had particularly painful memories of the 1965 series in the West Indies. He was an uncompromising man, both as captain and batsman, and was intent on grinding us into the ground. Under him were Ian Chappell and Walters, two fine young batsmen with an appetite for runs, backed up by Ian Redpath and Keith Stackpole. The bowling was spearheaded by Graham McKenzie, big Garth, who was very quick then, a fine bowler in any company. John Gleeson was a 'mystery' spinner who flicked the ball out of his fingers and who confused us for some time before we decided to treat him purely as an off-spinner.

Australia is a difficult place if you are doing poorly. The state sides are so strong that there is no chance for players out of form to get back their touch and for relaxation on the field, as there is in many county matches in England. The sun can be mercilessly hot and the outfields hard. For bowlers, the eight-ball over can be a killer, especially when the board reads, as we say at home, plenty for few – as it frequently did on that tour. And the Australians themselves have no sympathy. Their only object is to win and win at all costs.

Many years later a certain well-known Australian by the name of Kerry Packer told me that the good loser is the person who loses most often. He pretty fairly sums up the Australian attitude.

The strange thing was that we won the first Test at Brisbane by a clear margin. On reflection, it was probably the worst thing that could have happened, for it simply helped to heighten our complacency. If we had lost then as badly as we did later, we might have been forced into early corrective action.

I happened to make a significant contribution to the victory – with both bat and, if you please, ball! We were bowled out for 296 batting first, and Lawry and Chappell were both past their centuries with the total 200-odd for one when Sobers handed me the ball to try to winkle them out. They watched my gentle off-spin carefully at first and, having established that here were some cheap runs, decided to get after it. A risky thing that! Lawry holed out to midwicket, Chappell to cover, both to Gary, at which point he said thanks a lot, took away the ball and we were back in the game. The confidence trick had worked.

Now to batting. Up until then, I had had a bad time, struggling to get any runs, and I was worried. Sobers realized my concern and came across just before the match to say that the runs would come at the right time, not to bother. He had been through a similar bad patch on the 1960–1 trip and had come out of it with a century in the first Test.

The first innings did nothing to change my luck and I was out for 7. We were in trouble at 178 for six in the second when myself and Joey Carew came together. Like Chandrasekhar, Gleeson found he did not bowl as well to left-handers as to right- so that this left-handed partnership was to our advantage. I started poorly, largely because I was too hesitant, wanting too much to settle in. At least I survived and, after a while, began to feel the ball hit the middle of the bat again, a sweet sensation to anyone out of the runs. I went on to get 129, the last 100 of them in the final session of play, before McKenzie had me leg before with the second new ball by which time, with the pitch becoming increasingly worn, we were pretty securely placed.

I'm afraid that during the rest of the tour neither I nor the team approached our Brisbane form. We seemed always to be stretched out for days in the field with huge Australian totals against us. Just to make matters worse, I had to spend Christmas in bed in Melbourne with a very painful arm, caused when I was struck while fielding at cover in the South Australia match at Adelaide – my misery eased none as I listened to the West Indies slump to an innings defeat in the second Test at the MCG. Although I did manage to recover in time for the third Test, the rot had already set in for us and we were beaten at Sydney, too, by ten wickets.

Fortunately, we did manage to put up a marvellous performance in our second innings of the fourth Test at Adelaide. All our batsmen came off at just the right time to amass 616 and we then forced Australia to fight tooth and nail to stave off outright defeat, and they finished with nine second-innings wickets down. Since we had trailed by 257 on the first innings, it was a great recovery which did a lot for our sagging image and morale.

However, it was only a fleeting throwback to past glory and we were so badly outplayed in the final Test that Lawry, with absolutely no pity for the suffering we had undergone throughout the entire summer, declared his second innings to set us a small matter of 735 to win! This was just about the last straw and to be faced, after that, with another five weeks in New Zealand was too much to take.

By then, everyone was completely fed up and just going through the motions. There were one or two exceptions. Seymour Nurse batted like the maestro he was to score 95 and 168 in the first Test and a brilliant 258 not out in the third, Joey Carew continued his good Australian form, and Richard Edwards, who had been disappointing as one of the fast bowlers in Australia, adapted his style to suit the grassier pitches and took fifteen wickets in the three Tests. But everyone, without exception, wanted to get home.

Nurse, for instance, announced his retirement before the New Zealand series started, which might have accounted for his relaxed approach in the middle. Kanhai did not play at all because of an injured knee and said he would be unavailable for the forthcoming tour of England. And, to top things off, the team for the England tour was announced right in the middle of the second test at Wellington with Hall, Griffith, King and Edwards, the four fast bowlers, all omitted along with David Holford. Griff and Edwards reacted to the news with a spell of really fast and hostile bowling in that Test but by then it was too late.

New Zealand went on to win the match comfortably, and we had to return home with the further disappointment of a shared series with what was then considered the weakest team in Test cricket.

6 In the Doldrums, C.H. Lloyd

The five years between 1969 and 1973 were the most depressing of modern time for the West Indies in international cricket. After the ill-fated tour of Australia and New Zealand, we passed through four consecutive series without so much as a single Test victory to show. We lost 2–0 in England in 1969, 1–0 to India in the West Indies in 1971, were held to five draws by New Zealand at home in 1972, and then were beaten 2–0 by Ian Chappell's Australians, also at home, in 1973.

It is important to realize how much cricket means to West Indians. The game is followed with great fervour throughout the region; success or failure on the field of play by the Test team can dictate the mood of five million people. One has only to see the happy faces and watch the spring in the step of West Indians in England when their team is doing well in a Test match at Lord's or the Oval or wherever to appreciate the extent of their involvement.

So our failures during this period were unhappy experiences for our people – and, I might add, for our players as well, especially since they immediately followed the golden era when teams under Worrell and then Sobers were generally accepted as the best in the world. It was only to be expected, I suppose, that we would go into decline once the great players of the 1960s disappeared for it is impossible to replace men like Hall, Griffith, Hunte and Nurse in the twinkling of an eye. Yet we continued to contribute to our own troubles by lack of leadership, at all levels, by strange methods of selections and by the carping criticism which everyone was so quick to provide.

For me personally, it was a disheartening stage of my Test career. I went through three and a half series, four and a half years and twenty-three Tests without a Test century to my name. Everything seemed to go against me. I was not happy in the West Indies team, for several obvious reasons. I was run out an exceptional number of times and I sustained a serious back injury which, for a few anxious weeks, appeared likely to affect my career. When, in 1973, I was dropped out of the Test team, it was just about the last straw and I was so angry that I very nearly ended my days with the West Indies.

But one thing at a time; I will start with 1969 in England, the first trip there for the West Indies since the shared-tour arrangement had come in after our crowd-pulling performances of 1963 and 1966. This time, however, we had nothing like the teams we had then and we found it tough going, as everyone knew we would. There was no Hall, no Griffith, no Nurse, no Hunte, no Kanhai, no Holford – all experienced men out after the Australian and New Zealand tour. Instead, as many as eight of the sixteen were playing in England for the first time, and seven were in a West Indies team for the first time.

As if there was not enough going against us, the weather during May in the important build-up period was absolutely appalling, cold and wet most of the time and it was no wonder we were soundly beaten by ten wickets in the first Test at Manchester. Yet, all things considered, we did pretty well in the other two Tests. The second at Lord's was drawn with England, seven wickets down, still 37 away from their target and in the final Test, on a seamer's paradise at Headingley, only lack of experience prevented us winning, England taking a low-scoring match by 30 runs.

My own form was patchy, and the only Test innings of note was 70 in the second innings at Lord's. I was having problems handling the bouncer and was too inclined to hook it in the air. This was the first of many England tours on which Clyde Walcott was the manager, and he realized the hook was causing me to lose my wicket too often for my own good. So he talked to me and we discussed whether I would not be better off leaving out the shot altogether. In the end, we agreed. No more hooking – for a while at least – and I felt all the better for it.

However, this was another tour on which there was not enough discipline or discussion of tactics. The many young players were left to work things out on their own while certain senior individuals were picking and choosing their matches by opting out of teams on specious grounds. Someone even dropped out of a Test because of 'a pain' in his chest. When it comes to that it is not difficult to imagine what the spirit in the team was like.

Of course, the same thing had gone on in Australia and New Zealand not long before, so this was only a carry-over. In Australia, for instance, Stephen Camacho, a very talented young opening batsman, did not play a single game for something like two months, nursing some mysterious ailment. Yet he was allowed to stay on and no replacement asked for. That, in my opinion, was wrong.

Perhaps our woes were best summed up one July afternoon in Londonderry, where we had gone to play two one-day games against Ireland. We had been hurried over there the day after the Lord's Test, which was as thoughtless a piece of planning as any I have known, and we were in no mood for cricket on a pitch which, appropriately, was emerald green. Well, we got shot out for 25 – yes, 25 – and the press made a big song and dance about it. Our cricket had, surely, been taken over by the gremlins!

Thankfully, we had no Test commitments for a while after that tour and I was happy for the break. I had become disenchanted with Test cricket or, to be more accurate, with what was happening to the West Indies team. In contrast, the summer of 1970 was one of the most enjoyable of my career, playing for Lancashire under Jackie Bond for my first full season and taking part in the five Tests for the Rest of the World team against England, a series arranged as a substitute for the cancelled South African tour.

As I have stated earlier, Bond was a tremendous skipper and the Lancashire team enjoyed great success under him, winning both the John Player League and the Gillette Cup in that 1970 season and finishing third in the championship.

I had a great start with 163 against Kent at Dartford at something like a run-a-minute pace with seven sixes. It was one of those days when every shot came off. I can remember John Shepherd telling me before the match that Derek Underwood reckoned he had the ball to get me as he had noticed a weakness when he had played against me in a Derrick Robins game earlier in the season. Every time the ball soared out of the ground, Shep would pull Derek's leg by asking if that was the ball. Well, Underwood did finally get me out – and Shep couldn't help the comment: 'Ah, I knew you'd do him, Derek!' Yes, I enjoyed that innings and that season.

The World team was an extremely strong one – Barlow, Barry Richards, Kanhai, Graeme Pollock, Mushtaq Mohammad, Gary as captain, Mike Procter, Intikhab Alam, Lance Gibbs, Graham McKenzie, and Deryck Murray and Farokh Engineer sharing the wicketkeeping duties. What a team to be in. There were those who were sceptical as to whether the idea would work and it was sometime before the crowds started to come out. But we had a magnificent series, the cricket was played in a great spirit, although it was keen all the time, and I got 400 runs, including centuries at Trent Bridge and Edgbaston. Naturally, I looked forward to returning to the West Indies the following season for the 1971 visit of the Indians. Little did I anticipate the disappointments which were in store.

The long and short of it was that India won the only Test which was decided, taking the second at Port-of-Spain and then ensuring that they held us at bay in the rest. That bare recital of the fact of our defeat tells nothing of the torment through which our cricket passed in that season. India had never beaten us before, not in a series, not even in a Test, and the public felt that they should not have done so now. Even though the Indians possessed an excellent team, strong in batting and spin bowling and well led, to my mind the public was right. We were still in the stage of rebuilding and were not as strong as we were a few years earlier, yet we still had enough experience and all-round strength to have beaten them.

We lost not so much on the field – after all a single result decided the rubber – but off it. Again, we lacked direction and leadership and I'm not speaking about captaincy alone. We were assigned one manager in each Test centre, instead of one for the entire series, and he naturally could contribute little since he had not seen the previous Tests. The selection policy was again staggering and there was so much chopping and changing that only three of us – Sobers, Kanhai and myself – played in all the Tests; no fewer than twenty players played in the series. It got to the stage when you didn't know who your room-mate would be from match to match, and, of course, no one had that sense of stability which is so necessary for the confidence of any individual. In addition, we did not use the experienced players who would have made such a difference.

Lance Gibbs was played in only one Test and Jack Noreiga, a Trinidadian off-spinner, made his debut at the age of 35. He was something of a sensation, taking nine wickets in an innings in only his second Test and finishing with seventeen overall, but fifteen of them were on the spinner's pitch at the Queen's Park Oval. Holder, Keith Boyce and John Shepherd had all proven their worth in county cricket in England and, in the context of what was available at the time, would have brought much needed experience into the side. Yet Holder only played three Tests, Shepherd two and Boyce one on a featherbed of a pitch at Bourda.

In addition, Sobers came under great pressure for his captaincy. He had gone to Rhodesia to play in a tournament there after the English season and had been the centre of an enormous controversy because of it, which was only to be expected. Yet that had died down once the series started following a statement from Sobers. However, after India had won the second Test, criticism throughout the Caribbean was rampant and there were demands, especially from Trinidad who had won the Shell Shield for two consecutive seasons under Joey Carew, that Sobers be replaced. Let Carew take over, was the cry from Port-of-Spain. From everywhere else it was drop this one and drop that one as that old bugbear of West Indian cricket, insularity, reared its ugly head.

This only served to further deflate the morale of the team, and the Indians went from strength to strength, Sunil Gavaskar plundering our bowling at every turn in his very first series, with the experienced Dilip Sardesai not far behind.

Personally, it was almost as if there was some jinx preventing me getting a decent score. I was run out twice in the first Test, again in the second innings when I had gone past 50 and was feeling on top of the world, and then again in the first innings of the third, this time when I was 60.

The circumstances of that last run out were the most bizarre I have ever experienced on a cricket field and firmly convinced me that it was just not my season. I turned a ball behind square and, as fine leg had a long way to go to get it, sprinted the first and turned for an obvious second. Sobers was my partner and, as he came back up the pitch, he must have been looking behind him at the location of the ball. The next thing I knew was that he was on me and a front-on collision was inevitable. I went down as if hit by a Muhammed Ali right and, with wobbly knees, tried in vain to beat Bishen Bedi's return.

The incident typified the series from a West Indian point of view. There were several others which were similarly farcical.

In the first Test, for instance, rain had washed out the first day's play and reduced the match to four days, also reducing the follow-on figure from 200 to 150 runs. Yet, throughout our first innings, no one seemed aware of that change until it was too late and we were sent back in trailing by 170, much to everyone's embarrassment. Then, in the final Test at Port-of-Spain, there was the strange case of both captains claiming the toss. Gary spun the coin and was surprised when Wadekar said he would bat since he was sure the Indian skipper had called wrong. Some of the ground staff and one of the radio commentators who were around also believed the toss had gone to the West Indies. But Gary just shrugged his shoulders and made no issue of it – an indication of his sportsmanship. From my own point of view, however, I would have demanded at least a re-toss, particularly as it was such a vital match.

There is one story which, I believe, reveals the exasperation which had crept into our cricket. At the team meeting prior to the final Test, the talk got around to Gavaskar who, by this time, was a real problem. How should we get him out? There were several suggestions about how best to bowl to him but that of Lance Pierre, the former Trinidad and West Indies fast bowler who was match manager, topped the lot. We should, Lance said, bring him on the front foot, keep him quiet and then serve him up with a waist-high full toss which, in his anxiety to get it away, he would hit to deep square leg for a catch! Well, it was a novel argument, at least, although, I might add, we never tried it. Perhaps if we had employed this tactic Gavaskar would not have made 124 and 220 as he did in that game!

My return to England for the summer of 1971 put the

trials and tribulations of West Indian cricket at the back of my mind. In the more relaxed atmosphere of county cricket, the runs came again. In addition, Lancashire beat Kent in a most exciting Gillette Final at Lord's to climax another good year.

By then, I had been approached to join a World team to play in Australia as replacement for yet another cancelled South African trip and, naturally, I jumped at the opportunity. This one, however, was nothing near the strength of that which had played in England in 1970 and we struggled, particularly at Perth in the second Test when Dennis Lillee first came to international attention with a magnificent piece of really fast bowling on that WACA pitch which, then at least, was so quick. He got eight for 29 and we were skittled for 59 in our first innings, losing eventually by an innings. When we were beaten by an innings in the next match by South Australia our stocks were pretty low and so was public interest.

As it so happened that match was to be my last of the tour – and very nearly the last of my life.

Trying to make a catch at covers off Ashley Mallett in South Australia's first innings, I dived in goalkeeper-fashion and came crashing down on my shoulder. Almost as soon as I hit the ground, I knew something was seriously wrong. A stabbing pain went through my body and I just couldn't move. Tony Greig, who was fielding close by, came across and said something like: 'Come on, Lloydie, up you get, let's get on with it.' But my legs had no feeling and would not move. It was soon evident to everyone that it was a severe injury, a stretcher was sent for and I was whisked away to hospital.

It was a month before I was released – one of the most agonizing times of my life, both mentally and physically. It took a few hours before a tingling feeling started to return to my legs and a few weeks of meticulous physiotherapy treatment before I could walk again. During this time I had a surging, excruciating pain throughout my body, dulled only by the many tablets I was given.

The problem, according to the excellent doctor, Dr Baird, who treated me, was a small crack at the base of the spine. If I had fallen any heavier, or at a slightly different angle, he said, it would have been much worse.

It is difficult to explain my state of mind during that period, especially early on before I knew the full extent of the damage. The accident occurred on 17 December and I had only been married in October. How was the news going to affect Waveney, thousands of miles away in Manchester? Cricket was my life. When would I be able to play again? Would I *ever* be able to play again? How would it affect my movements if I did return?

I was lucky in many respects. The injury was not as bad as at first imagined, and the staff at the hospital and cricketing friends in Adelaide, such as the Chappells and Ashley Mallett, paid regular visits to cheer me up. I had one of the best rooms in the hospital and, with all the liquid Christmas presents I received, I could have opened an off-licence and done a roaring trade.

With such tender loving care, I was literally back on my feet again within a month and was able to return to the West Indies by early February 1972. By then, the New Zealanders had started their first tour of the Caribbean and I knew it would take some time before I was ready to play. In the meantime, a young Jamaican by the name of Lawrence Rowe was making a sensational debut to his Test career with 214 and 100 not out in his first Test in Kingston – but the New Zealanders were proving they would be no push-over.

I took my first tentative steps on to a cricket field again in the Shield match against Barbados in Georgetown on 26 February, scored 60 and realized that there was nothing to worry about. As far as the West Indies selectors were concerned, however, I needed to do a little more to get back my place; only after I scored centuries in each innings in Guyana's match against the New Zealanders was I reinstated. By then, three Tests had been drawn, two of them in New Zealand's favour, and the public was as despondent as they had been the previous season against India.

For me, it was if nothing had changed and my first Test innings on return to the West Indies side ended in yet another run out – one which caused more trouble than simply my dismissal. I drove Howarth, the left-arm spinner, to mid-off and went for the single, only to find that Charlie David at the opposite end had not moved. There was no hope of getting back and, yet again, *run out* went next to my name in the book. I was 43 at the time and, as I was playing at home and there would have been a number of bets about me getting to 50 or 100, the incident caused an angry outburst from some sections of the crowd.

Bottles were hurled on to the field and poor Charlie was abused left, right and centre and, later, advised to stay in his hotel that night for his own safety, although I am sure that was over-reacting. However, I had to go to the radio commentary position to broadcast an appeal to the crowd and, after twenty minutes, calm was restored.

That Test – with Glenn Turner scoring 259 and adding 387 for the first wicket with Terry Jarvis – was drawn, as was the last Test, and scores of 18 and 5 in the final Test did not help me to reassert myself in the minds of our selectors. In fact, when they came to announce the customary list of names of professionals to be retained for the following series against Australia in the West Indies in 1973, that of C.H. Lloyd was nowhere to be found. If I wanted my position back I would have to return from England at my own expense and fight for it along with everyone else in the Shell Shield.

The decision upset me greatly. I had become disillusioned with Test cricket in any case and I now felt under no obligation to the West Indies. When a contract to play club cricket for South Melbourne in Australia for the 1972–3 season was offered as a replacement for Tony Greig, I accepted, even though I knew it would effectively eliminate me from playing at home. After all, the selectors had made their decision and I now had to make mine.

Matters developed quickly following the selectors' announcement. 1972 was not a particularly happy season for me, and I think the after-effects of the back trouble sustained in Australia contributed to my absence for several matches from the Lancashire team through illness and injury. However, I enjoyed a most pleasing climax to that year, an innings of 126 at Lord's which helped Lancashire win the Gillette Cup Final by four wickets over Warwickshire. It earned me the Man of the Match Award and, I believe, also caused some embarrassment to the President of the West Indies Board, Cecil Marley.

Cecil Marley was in England at the time, saw the innings

and came across to me afterwards to say that he would have to report back to the selectors and try to get them to change their decision not to recall me. In addition, four West Indian Test players were on the opposing side that day – Rohan Kanhai, Alvin Kallicharran, Deryck Murray and Lance Gibbs – and, as it turned out, Kanhai was to be chosen as captain for the Australian series. So I think, one way or another, I had made a point even if I had not consciously set out to do so. I did strike the ball well that day and the press was most flattering in its description of the strokeplay.

A little later on, I received a letter from Jeffrey Stollmeyer, then Chairman of the selectors, asking me to stand by since Sobers, who was retained for the Australian series, was recovering from knee operations and was in some doubt. Even then, Gary had relinquished the captaincy and there was speculation over who would replace him. Kanhai, David Holford, the Barbadian skiper, and myself were tipped as the most likely candidates. But how could they choose me if I wasn't around?

It was a question which did not bother me much but it did bother the Prime Minister of Guyana, Forbes Burnham, who proceeded to have me return home from Australia so that I *would* be around. He wrote to the Prime Minister of Australia, Gough Whitlam, a personal friend, asking him to use his influence to have South Melbourne release me, an unusual step to say the least.

Since there were only a few more grade matches to be played and we had no chance of the title in any case, South Melbourne agreed. Perhaps they felt they were not losing much, as I had not got many runs for them and had proved more useful as a medium pacer! Whatever the reason, I was back in Manchester by early January and was called by the Guyana High Commissioner in London, Sir John Carter, to be told that the government would pay my passage back home. To be perfectly honest, I was a little apprehensive about accepting for I realized it would be interpreted as political interference in some quarters. However, if the Prime Minister of my country felt so strongly about it and wanted me home to play, at least for Guyana, the least I could do was to accept his generous offer.

So I was back home, sponsored, as it were, by the Guyana

government – and was quickly included in the West Indies squad for the first Test. I had had three matches by then – two in the Shield and one as captain of the President's XI against the Australians – and had done nothing of note, so I was not altogether surprised when I was omitted from the eleven for the first Test. We went on to Barbados for the second Test and, this time, I was named in the twelve from whom the final team would be selected.

As things turned out, Bernard Julien was injured while batting in the nets the day before the match and I took it that this would leave me automatically in the final eleven. I was astounded, therefore, when Jeffrey Stollmeyer, came across to me while I was knocking up on the outfield before start of play to advise that I would be twelfth man since Keith Boyce had been called in to replace Julien.

That did it. I was furious and, what with everything that had gone on over recent years in West Indies cricket, I erupted. I slammed the ball so hard that it crashed through one of the windows in our dressing room and when I got inside I broke down and cried out of pure anger and frustration. No, I would not be twelfth man, I told Clyde Walcott, who was the manager. No, I would not go out and meet the Governor-General in the team line. All I wanted was my plane ticket back to England because, as far as I was concerned, I was finished. I felt I was being victimized for the fact that Forbes Burnham had brought me back home and, my reasoning perhaps clouded by emotion, I wanted no further part of West Indies cricket.

Fortunately, two men for whom I have a great deal of respect influenced me into calming down and seeing things in a different light. Clyde Walcott, who could so easily have just walked away, talked sensibly, telling me that I had a great future in West Indies cricket, that I could contribute a lot as I was still a young man, and urged me not to throw it away. Later, Wes Hall came in and said much the same thing, coaxing me into seeing reason. Wes pointed out that I had been chosen to lead the President's XI and that Rohan was nearing the end of his career and would not have long as skipper.

Two and two always make four, even in West Indies cricket, and I got the message. Future events proved how

62

right both Clyde and Wes were. It is interesting to realize that many of those very young and inexperienced players who were under me in that President's team were to become the stalwarts in the West Indies team I would eventually lead – Gordon Greenidge, Vivian Richards, Bernard Julien, David Murray and Mike Holding.

So I cooled down, kept my place in the squad and finally got selected for the third Test at the Queen's Park Oval. Because of the nature of the pitch, we concentrated heavily on spin and I was required to open the bowling with my gentle medium-pace. It was a wonderful match, played in gripping tension throughout, with Australia winning by 44 runs. We batted without one of our main batsmen, Lawrence Rowe, who injured an ankle in the field on the first day and although that proved a terrible handicap, we played and fought well.

For my own part, however, I struggled to make 20 and 15 and the Trinidadian public was quick to stick in the knives with their usual hurtful criticism – criticism which shocked poor Waveney who was on holiday and was watching from the stands. She had not seen much cricket in the Caribbean and was now learning!

It was at Bourda that I finally laid my troubles to rest. I had been giving contact lenses a try for some time but they had been so dusted up on an almost grassless Queen's Park Oval that I decided to return to the old specs for the Guyana match against the tourists. Whether it was that or the fact that I felt at home in Georgetown, I don't know but I scored 124 in the first innings and went into the Test with confidence – though still feeling I had to do something special to prove to the Guyanese public that the money spent on my return by the government was worth it.

By the end of the first day, I had 139 to my name and, next day, went on to reach 178, my highest Test score at the time. We were off to an excellent start at 269 for three on the first day and, even though we declined to 366 all out on the second, I knew I had done my part in putting us in a good position.

We actually led by 25 on first innings but then collapsed, on a good pitch, so disastrously in the second innings that we were 109 all out and the Australians went on to win by ten wickets and so put a seal on the series. This astounding and most disheartening reversal yet again threw West Indian cricket into a state of melancholy. When we went back to Trinidad for the final Test, the vast stands which had been filled to capacity for the third Test were virtually empty. After a steady succession of defeats and almost endless controversy over one problem after another, West Indian cricket was on its knees and its ever-faithful public, prepared to take no more, had started to desert it.

Fortunately, happy times were just around the corner.

7 The Test Captaincy

Even though the West Indies were beaten in the series against Australia at home early in 1973, our performance was not as bad as it appeared on the surface. We might well have won the Trinidad Test and we were beaten in Guyana on the one poor batting display we suffered for the series. However, people are interested only in good results and we had not provided them with any for a long, long time.

That was to change in England in 1973 when West Indies cricket was revitalized with our emphatic triumph over England by two wins and a draw in the three Tests series. The clouds which had hung so heavily over West Indian cricket for more than five long years now lifted and a bright new future lay ahead.

It is difficult to put a finger on any one factor which was responsible for the sudden revival. Rather, it was a combination. I think the change of captaincy did make a difference. It was not that Kanhai was any better tactically than Sobers. They were, in fact, direct opposites in their methods. While Sobers was an attacking skipper, always willing to take a chance in an effort to win, Kanhai was cautious and defensive. The perfect skipper, I felt, would have been a blend of the two, for Sobers tended to take too many risks and Kanhai not enough.

The main difference, for that series at least, was interest and commitment. Towards the end of his days of captaincy, Sobers had lost his appetite for leadership and, as I have pointed out before, let things drift. When Kanhai was appointed as his successor, there were several raised eyebrows, for he did not have an exactly saintly reputation in his many years of international cricket. Yet he brought a sense of responsibility to the job and his total involvement communicated itself to the rest of the team.

We were suddenly talking more about the game, having more meaningful team meetings and, in general, having a sense of belonging to a unit. Kanhai may not have been the most popular individual with his players, and I also got the feeling that some of the younger ones held him in awe. Yet he did achieve something.

In addition, it was a tremendous advantage to us that the majority of our players were now engaged in county cricket in England so that we knew the conditions and our opponents, their strengths and weaknesses, intimately. Only two of those who played in the Tests, Inshan Ali and Maurice Foster, were not county professionals and they had only one Test each. Even when we lost our opener, Camacho, who was hit, ironically, by Andy Roberts, in the match against Hampshire, we could bring in a replacement of vast experience of England, Ron Headley. It was a strong all-round combination, strengthened even further by the welcome return for the Tests of the greatest of them all, Gary Sobers.

For my own part, the worrying problems which had confronted me with such frequency in the preceding few years were now all behind me. I was a senior member and was appointed a tour selector and a member of the tour committee. This was in June and I could not help reflecting what Clyde Walcott and Wes Hall had said to me in the dressing room at Kensington Oval only three months earlier when I was so intent on abandoning West Indian cricket.

As with almost every other endeavour in this world, state of mind is vital to the performance of a cricketer and so it proved with me. The weather was generally good and so were the pitches, the team was keen and committed to doing well and it only followed that I would get some runs. As it happened, I scored well in every Test – 130 at the Oval in the first, 94 in the second at Edgbaston and 63 in the last at Lord's.

The first was the most memorable – and not just because it was the highest. We were in trouble when Kallicharran joined me at 64 for three with Geoff Arnold and John Snow moving the ball all over the place under grey skies in the morning session. However, the sun broke through after lunch; suddenly the ball stopped moving and we had a partnership of over 200 which, in the context of the match and the series as a whole, was important. In addition, it was my first Test century in England.

The other innings were less significant for the Edgbaston match ended in a draw and 63 out of 652 for eight declared, our total at Lord's, was hardly worthy of notice.

Individually, however, that series belonged to Keith Boyce. He had done great things for Essex for several seasons but there were those (apparently including the West Indies selectors) who doubted whether he was up to international level since he tended to be a little erratic. Yet he bowled with real fire throughout, taking eleven wickets at the Oval and eight at Lord's in the Tests we won; he also hit the ball like thunder, and fielded and threw magnificently in the deep. He is not a big man by any means but he was a bundle of energy and always ready to give 100 per cent effort. Our manager, Esmond Kentish, used to refer to him as his 'Pocket Hercules' and I think that just about summed him up.

There were other wonderful moments. The batting of Fredericks at Edgbaston when he put his head down, curbed his natural game and battled through for almost a day and a half for 150 – only to be castigated by an English press which didn't seem to appreciate the value of the innings. And then there were the centuries by Kanhai and Sobers at Lord's, vintage stuff from two great players in their farewell Test appearances in England – a fitting finale at a fitting venue, Sobers lending additional sparkle with six superb close-to-the-wicket catches. Then there was Bernard Julien's maiden Test century at Lord's which, along with his left-arm swing bowling, convinced everyone of his enormous potential. Unfortunately, he did not seem to be convinced himself and his subsequent downward slide has been an inexplicable waste of talent.

There were other memories, too, not so happy. One concerned the incident at Edgbaston when we appealed for a catch at the wicket from Boycott, always our main target. When umpire Arthur Fagg refused it, a lot of our players predictably reacted angrily. I cannot say whether Fagg was abused or not because I was nowhere near, but I do feel that he was over-reacting when he refused to take the field the next day until we issued an apology. If all umpires took that attitude, there would have to be a staff of reserves in every Test. It is not that I condone verbal abuse of umpires. They have a difficult job at the best of times and, unlike referees in soccer or hockey, do not have the authority to send players off. Yet, in the tension of international cricket, they must expect players to react to their decision. Players are only human and, even so, in all my career, I have never felt their reactions were overdone.

Then there was the bomb scare at Lord's. It was inevitable, I suppose, that some crackpot would choose a Test match as a target to get his kicks and what better place than Lord's. We were in the field at the time when the announcement came for the stands to be cleared and, personally, I never felt in any danger. But it was a nuisance.

The only scares the Englishmen got on their tour to the West Indies a few months later were from the explosions of Lawrence Rowe's bat. The stylish Jamaican had not played Test cricket since his accident during the third Test of the series against Australia the previous season and he hardly did anything on his return in the first Test at Trinidad.

However, he was soon in his best form with 120 in the second Test in front of his worshippers at Sabina Park, then 302 at Kensington Oval and, finally, 128 at the Queen's Park Oval in the last Test. He really was in tremendous form and there is no better sight in the game than Rowe at his best.

All the other batsmen had to take a back seat to Rowe, and I only managed one score over 50 in the entire series. There was no doubt that we had a far better team and we outplayed England in the first three Tests. But we could only press home our advantage in the first, which we won, and they managed to level things by winning the final Test in Trinidad where Tony Greig bowled his off-spinners magnificently to take thirteen wickets on a typically helpful pitch.

This disappointing result for the West Indies was probably the main factor in causing the selectors to relieve Kanhai of the captaincy. During that series, I think the strain of the job began to tell on him, and he was finding it difficult to concentrate for any length of time while batting. Nevertheless, most people felt he would be retained for the tour to India, Sri Lanka and Pakistan which was to follow late in the year. Certainly I thought so, and was taken by surprise when Howard Booth, the *Daily Mirror* cricket correspondent, rang me during a Lancashire match against Yorkshire at Leeds during the summer to congratulate me on my appointment as the new West Indies captain. It was a

68

strange way to learn one of the most important pieces of news in my life, and it was not until some time afterwards that official notification came from the West Indies Board.

Naturally, I was elated. It must be the dream of most young boys to captain their country at cricket and I know it was mine. The first thing I did was to call my wife to share the news with her, and then I went out with some of the Lancashire lads for a few celebration drinks.

Many things ran through my mind during the rest of that summer about the assignment which had been given to me. More than anything, I told myself, I wanted to instil a sense of discipline into the teams I would skipper. I had seen too many West Indian teams, full of natural talent, suffer because of a lack of it. In addition, I felt it important to communicate to players the need for fitness, another aspect of the game which I had found wanting in West Indian cricket, and of the importance of winning.

There were other factors which I had to consider, such as speech-making, the personal relationships with players and the conduct of team meetings. On the field, tactics, I felt, would take care of themselves for I had not played the game for so long without forming opinions about how to deal with given situations, even though I had not had much experience of captaincy – a match at Scarborough with the West Indies in 1973, that President's XI game in 1973 and a few games with Guyana. However, during that 1974 summer, I had the opportunity to skipper Lancashire several times while David Lloyd, who had only taken over that year, was on duty in the Tests against India and Pakistan.

It was, in fact, a blank summer for Lancashire since we won nothing.

Yet we did reach the semi-finals of the Benson and Hedges Cup and the final of the Gillette, in which we were beaten by Kent, and I enjoyed the additional responsibility of the captaincy. A total of 1403 runs at an average of over 63 was just enough to put me in the right frame of mind for the winter series in India and Pakistan.

My main worries before we set out was the length of the tour, from the first week of November to the second week of March, the distances we had to travel and the effect conditions would have on the young players, so many of whom were on their first trip with the West Indies.

Those worries all proved unfounded. Naturally, there were a few times when one or two individuals would get depressed and home-sick, particularly as we spent the Christmas period in India, and there were a few grumbles early on about the food and the standard of accommodation in some of the smaller venues.

All in all, however, it was a wonderful tour. We won an exciting series in India 3–2, had the better of the two Tests in Pakistan and there was not a single individual in the group who could have been deemed a failure – a rare occurrence.

As captain, I was genuinely lucky with the assistance of those who formed the tour committee – manager, Gerry Alexander, vice-captain, Deryck Murray, and the senior player, Lance Gibbs.

Gerry, to be straight to the point, was the best manager I have ever encountered in a West Indies team. I had not met him before the team assembled in London but, naturally, knew him by reputation, a former West Indies skipper himself, and a wicketkeeper and batsman with a fine Test record.

We seemed to hit it off from the very start. Gerry would get totally involved with every situation concerning the team. He was not overly concerned about the social side of things and the diplomatic protocol as it were, although he did not neglect them. But he made every member of the team feel that he had their interest at heart.

He imposed the discipline necessary without being a dictator, and he had a most effective way of bringing out those players who were reluctant to speak on cricketing matters. He would play devil's advocate, putting forward some outrageous point of view that was bound to stir a counter-argument from the most placid of individuals. Yet he never over-stepped the mark or entered what he considered the captain's territory. If he wanted to speak to the team on some matter he would come to me first. And he did everything himself, without the benefit of an assistant manager or treasurer.

The fact that everyone contributed to our success can be gauged from the averages. Our five major batsmen all scored over 300 in the Tests – and Baichan and Julien, who played in only a few Tests, got centuries against Pakistan – and our five main bowlers all took ten wickets or more in the Tests.

What was most gratifying was the role played by three new players, Andy Roberts, Vivian Richards and Gordon Greenidge.

Roberts had played one Test against England the previous season and had done great things for Hampshire in his first full season with them. He was young, strong and deceptively quick and he provided the genuine pace which our attack had lacked for some time. When the seven Tests were over, he had forty-six wickets to his name.

His fellow Antiguan, Richards, was one of the most enthusiastic cricketers I had seen and, if he was a little impetuous, he had enormous potential. Even after he failed in the first Test, out both times to Chandrasekhar, we persisted with him because it was obvious he was something special. He rewarded our faith with a magnificent 192 not out in the second Test at Delhi. In addition, he was sensational in the field and took two catches at short leg in the first Test that I will never forget.

Greenidge had made his reputation in England playing for Hampshire and he now settled the problem of Fredericks's partner which had troubled the West Indies for a long time. In the years to come, all three – Roberts, Richards and Greenidge – were to be key members of the West Indies team.

There is a body of opinion that captaincy can effect a cricketer's overall performance – a batsman's batting, a bowler's bowling – but I have never understood the theory behind it. If anything, captaincy adds a sense of responsibility to the individual and my own batting seemed to prosper because of it. That series in India was the best of my career – 636 runs all told, with 163 in the first Test at Bangalore and 242 not out at Bombay, my highest in not only Test cricket but all first-class cricket as well, in the last.

My major problem seemed to be with the toss, for I called wrongly every time in the first four Tests. Not that the toss mattered in the first two. In the first at Bangalore, we had to bat first after being sent in on a pitch which was affected by rain and also the strange Indian regulation that it remain uncovered throughout. That we reached 289 was due to a

71

remarkable innings of 124 by Kallicharran and 93 run out in his first Test innings by Greenidge. We managed a narrow lead on first innings, and the match was evenly balanced when we were three down for 75 in our second innings. By then, however, the wicket had become easier and Greenidge and myself put on 207 for the fourth wicket which just about clinched things, especially since India were unlucky in having to bat without their two most experienced players, Engineer and skipper Pataudi, in the second innings through injury.

When the second Test went our way by an innings, Lance Gibbs exploiting a wicket again affected by rain India's second innings, there was no doubt that our players became a little complacent. It is a real danger with any team which wins so comfortably and was reflected in the fact that we dropped several catches in our very next game against Central Zone up at Nagpur.

I could sense the problem and ordered intensive fielding and catching practice prior to the third Test at Calcutta, while also trying to impress on everyone that the series was far from over. By the time the fourth Test was over, the series was, in fact, very much alive with India having drawn level at 2–2.

Our batsmen probably were a little too cocky in their approach at the start of the third Test when we were bowled out for 240, of which Roy Fredericks made an even 100 with a typically courageous performance. However, that brought everyone back to earth and complacency could not be blamed for what happened thereafter. Instead, the toss proved crucial at both Calcutta and Madras where the pitches broke up; we had bad luck with a few important run outs (Richards at Calcutta and Kallicharran at Madras), and a few key umpiring decisions went against us.

In addition, the Indians played very well. They had a good skipper in Pataudi, while little Vishwanath proved he was a batsman of true world class, and the spin trio of Bedi, Chandrasekhar and Prasanna revelled in conditions which helped them. Gavaskar was on the injured list so one of the pillars of the Indian batting was absent but the other one, Viswanath, more than compensated for his loss. In those two Tests which India won his scores were 52 out of 233, 139 out of 316, 97 out of 190 and 46 out of 256, which is outstanding by any standards.

When we came to Bombay for the decisive final Test, there were rumours that the pitch was underprepared and would not last the distance of six days. The stadium was new and not many matches had been played on the ground, so no one was certain what conditions would be like. It was a very tense West Indies captain who took the field to toss before the start because I felt that a correct call would decide the match. When I did call and the coin dropped in my favour, I think the sigh of relief could be heard by the 60,000 Indians in the ground. As it turned out, I need not have bothered; the pitch played beautifully all the way through and was one of the best I have played on.

When we ended the first day 309 for three, I knew that we were in command. I was already past 50 when the second day started and I continued on and on, feeling in very good form and hitting the ball pretty well. I went past 200 and really felt that I could have got to 300 that day had not a crowd riot halted play. What happened was that a lone spectator, a young lad in his teens, jumped the fence and came on to shake my hand after I got 200. Since it was not a massive invasion, I thought nothing of it, but the police had other ideas. In front of everyone they used their long bamboo sticks, the *lahtis*, with a vengeance on the poor boy and incensed the crowd to such an extent that, by tea, there was a full-scale riot which left the place looking like a battlefield.

We remained in our dressing room and were never in any danger. However, an hour and a half's play had been lost and, since we were so well placed, it was only obvious that we would ask for the time to be made up on subsequent days. The Indian Board refused that request and, as it turned out, we did not require the time.

I finally declared after Deryck Murray and myself had added 250 for the sixth wicket and we set about trying to win by an innings. However, the Indians made us fight harder than we expected. The left-handed Solkar got a century; Viswanath and Gavaskar, now recovered, got among the runs; and the follow-on was saved by a few runs. However, a fine spell by that old workhorse Vanburn Holder in the second innings, when he took six wickets, clinched it for us.

What sticks out in my memory about that Test even more than our victory and my own score was the finale. We had got back into our dressing room when someone came in and said the crowd was chanting for us to make a farewell appearance in the middle. We all came out, the full squad along with the manager, and we walked to the pitch to the cheering of the spectators all of whom seemed to have remained in the ground for the occasion. It was an emotional and unforgettable moment.

Perhaps it would have been better to have ended the tour there and then, but we still had another six weeks in front of us in Sri Lanka and Pakistan. This was simply too much and, even though we had two excellent and keenly contested drawn Tests in Pakistan, we were all pretty happy when it was all over and we could get back home.

We were tired men by then and, although the Shell Shield lay ahead, it is not an exacting tournament and I looked on it as a kind of occupational therapy. That I could lead Guyana to the title in my first season as captain rounded things off nicely as far as I was concerned before I was off to England for another year with Lancashire – and the first World Cup.

8   Sweet and Sour

Cricket, I have often heard it said, is a great leveller. One moment you are up, the next you are down and then you are up again. There is no player, even the greatest, who has not had to endure the feeling of disappointment during his career and to learn to accept the good times with the bad.

I speak from experience for my fortunes seemed to go up and down like a yo-yo from the very start, but never more so than in the early 1970s. There was that back injury in Adelaide in 1971 and the omission from the West Indies team in 1973 which left me so despondent I was on the verge of giving up Test cricket altogether. Then, suddenly, the sun peeped out from behind the clouds and everything was bright again. My own form was excellent and I was appointed West Indies captain for a tour of India, Sri Lanka and Pakistan which I rate as one of the happiest I have been on.

When I arrived in Manchester to report for the 1975 season with Lancashire the world seemed a wonderful place and playing cricket just about the best thing imaginable. It was a season in which the game's first World Cup tournament would be staged, in England, for a fortnight in June and I was looking forward to that as much as anything else, since the West Indies would have an excellent chance.

As it turned out, 1975 was the most memorable year I have ever spent in England. For Lancashire, I scored six centuries in a total of 1390 runs and got 73 not out in beating Middlesex in the Gillette Cup Final at Lord's. Of more international importance, the West Indies captured the World Cup in a really wonderful competition which surpassed even the wildest expectations of the organizers – and to top it off, I took the Man of the Match Award in the Final against Australia following an innings of 102 and twelve fairly respectable overs of medium-pace which, since my League days, had become my stock-in-trade as a bowler.

We had been made favourites before the competition started and this was probably justifiable. Most of our players had plenty of experience of one-day cricket with the counties and we were very well served with all-rounders and good fielders with strong throwing arms. Yet England, playing at home, could not be underestimated. Pakistan also had a strong team with plenty of English experience, and Australia, although relatively new to this type of game, would never be an easy proposition.

In addition, we had a difficult draw in the preliminary round with both Australia and Pakistan in our section, along with the weaker Sri Lanka. We started with a comfortable win over Sri Lanka at Old Trafford and then went down to Edgbaston for the game against Pakistan. And what a game it was!

We didn't bowl very well, and the strong Pakistani batting rattled up 266 for seven from the allotted sixty overs. Conditions were perfect and we had the batting to knock that off but something went wrong somewhere along the line and it was a very quiet dressing room when Vanburn Holder walked out to join Deryck Murray at 166 for eight. Fingers were crossed and a few silent prayers were said but I do not honestly believe any one of us held out much hope of victory. After all, the age of miracles had long gone.

There was at least one exception. My acountant, Gordon Andrews, a member of Warwickshire, had put something like £50 on us to win. That was a lot to put on a game of cricket and I told him so. Perhaps I was feeling a little guilty at our showing, but *his* spirits never flagged. He brought a crate of ale into the dressing room and, as the Murray – Holder partnership began to flourish, I could sense the tension rising. Vannie went and Andy Roberts joined Murray, the last pair at the wicket and still 64 needed.

Run by run the target came closer and closer and we got noisier and noisier in the dressing room, cheering every shot like excited schoolboys. The Pakistanis began to panic and, the more they did, it seemed the cooler Deryck and Andy, who are two unflappable customers at the best of times, became. Bottles started to disappear from the crate of ale faster and faster and when, against all the odds, Andy pushed Wasim Raja into the leg-side for the winning run with two balls remaining, the scenes were incredible.

West Indians in the crowd mobbed Deryck, and it was some time before he could get inside to join the celebrations and receive his deserved congratulations. In all my days of playing cricket, I have never known such elation in a dressing room. Some years later, when we won a similarly close World Series Cricket match in Australia, there was great jubilation but it wasn't quite as emotional. Men with years of cricket experience were jumping up and down and hugging each other. Several were sobbing uncontrollably. And don't get the idea that I was all calm and dignified through it all. I did a bit of hugging and shouting myself.

That was a very important win. After that, I believe the team as a whole knew that it would not be stopped and would win the Cup. It was the type of performance which helped to erase the age-old feeling that the West Indies were no good fighting from behind.

We advances to the semi-finals with a straightforward victory over Australia on a very slow pitch at the Oval which was in our favour, with Kallicharran hooking and cutting Lillee and Thomson to the delight of the thousands of West Indians who were there to shout us on. After defeating New Zealand in the semis, it was to be another clash with Australia in the final.

We had been fortunate throughout the tournament with the weather. On 2 June snow had stopped play in a county match yet, for the fortnight of the Cup, it was gloriously sunny and warm. It was suggested that the weather suited us but, in fact, it suited the entire competition.

The final itself was blessed with the same conditions, and I was a little surprised when Ian Chappell won the toss and put us in. The pitch looked a real beauty and, with our batting, I felt a total of 250 was on the cards. Having played Australia in the semi-final, we planned carefully how to bowl to them, deciding to concentrate on or just outside their off-stumps since they were such good players through the on-side.

We did not start as confidently as I had hoped, and I was walking out at 50 for three with Fredericks, Greenidge and Kallicharran all gone. In limited-over cricket, we had always considered a good, solid start as important so I was a little apprehensive. However, conditions were made to order for batting and everything went right.

With the absence of spin, bowling in one-day cricket lacks variety, and that day the pitch did nothing for the quick bowlers and everything for the batsmen. The ball was coming off the middle of the bat virtually from the first shot and, as sometimes happens, I suspected that this would by my day.

When I was finally given out (I use the term advisedly), caught down the leg-side by Marsh off Gilmour, for 102, we were 199 for four and I was confident that we would not lose from there. It is always stimulating to receive a standing ovation on returning to the pavilion, but doubly so when that pavilion happens to be at Lord's and the occasion one so distinguished as the first World Cup Final. The noise of the crowd is mostly lost when you are in the middle concentrating on the job at hand and it is only at intervals during a big innings – such as reaching 50 or 100 or at the end of it – that most batsmen have time to savour the applause.

I have been asked many times how I rate that particular innings. The truth is that comparisons, as someone once said, are odious. Factors such as conditions, the quality of the bowling, the occasion and so on must be taken into account. It is enough to say it was one of the most enjoyable knocks I can remember playing.

It would not have been possible without the support throughout of Rohan Kanhai, a great batsman whose enormous experience and technique ensured that our recovery from early difficulties was complete. He scored less than 50 at the other end while I passed my century, but this was just the type of role which was needed. In fact, it was his last innings for the West Indies and he can hardly have played many more important.

Once we had totalled as many as 291 for eight off our sixty overs, we had the match sewn up, although we had to guard against complacency. As it was, the Australians fought to the end and produced a really exciting match for a full house. In all our preparations, we laid great emphasis on fielding for we all appreciated how vital it was, and this paid off in the end. The Australians were forced to take chances throughout and we had five run outs in all, three of them claimed by Richards. Since two of them were the Chappell brothers, who to us were as dangerous as the James brothers used to be in the Wild West, it was a major contribution to our effort.

The sensation of holding the Prudential Trophy aloft after it had been presented by Prince Phillip is difficult to describe. The hundreds of West Indians who gathered in front of the pavilion to hail the victory emphasized how much it meant to them: there would be great rejoicing back home as well. The prevalent emotions were, understandably, pride and joy and, although I am not an emotional person, it was a very moving moment which I will always cherish.

I think we all had a little too much to drink that night and, from what I understood afterwards, hangovers were a common complaint of most West Indian cricket followers the morning after. I was more than a little disappointed, therefore at the Board's response – or lack of it – to our success. The team members never received any recognition from the Board, apart from the agreed fee of £350, and this left a somewhat bitter feeling. In this regard, its dealing with the players, the administration has been lacking and, as every large organization now appreciates, personal relations are an important aspect in any efficient operation. A special ceremony, a special match, anything to show that it meant something to the Board would have been appreciated. Instead it was left to the Guyana government to fly me back home with the Trophy for motorcades through the streets of Georgetown and to present every member of the team with a commemorative gold chain. Later, the Caribbean governments agreed to mark the occasion with special stamps. But that was about all. I can just imagine how the players of India or Pakistan or Australia would have been fêted at home had they won the Cup.

The result of that World Cup tournament and the Test series in India and Australia the preceding seasons prompted unprecedented interest in the West Indies tour of Australia in 1975–6 for six Tests. We had done well enough in India and Parkistan while Australia was defeating England 4–1 in Australia for the media to dub our forthcoming encounter as a 'world championship'.

I wrote in a newspaper column before that series that there was not much between the two teams where talents and skills were involved and I predicted the outcome could 'hang on a slender thread'. I still stand by that assessment although we suffered a thorough thrashing by 5–1.

Most observers agree, even now, that the overall result was not a fair reflection of the standards of the teams. In fact, the series was a very even contest until about half-way through.

Australia won the first Test by eight wickets, a comfortable enough margin on paper but which, in effect, was a tough fight for them. We batted poorly in our first innings to be out for 214, yet we recovered so well with centuries from Rowe and Kallicharran that they had a target of 219 in the final innings of the match on a wearing pitch. Lance Gibbs bowled magnificently and we only needed to separate those dreaded Chappell brothers early on to have had a good chance of breaking through. We had the chance when Inshan Ali dropped a return off Ian relatively early in his innings, but that was it. Greg completed two centuries in the match and both were still not out when the winning run was scored.

We went on to Perth, where Roberts and Holding bowled really fast, where Fredericks blazed 169 with some of the most exciting strokes I have ever witnessed, and where I scored 149 in our total of 585. With Roberts taking seven wickets in their second innings, Australia were routed for 169 and we won by an innings and 87 runs.

Lillee and Thomson, who had created terrible havoc on England the previous season, both had centuries against their names at the end of our innings; Thomson had taken only four wickets at that stage, and there was some talk that he might be dropped. We were really confident then that we would win the series – Roberts and Holding, in his very first series, formed a hostile striking force; Rowe, Kallicharran, Fredericks and myself had all scored centuries, and the Australians seemed worried.

So what made us lose the following four Tests all very conclusively? There were a variety of reasons and I will try to list them.

Before I am accused of offering lame excuses, let me say that the Australians deserved their success. They were the better team in the series, they applied themselves better and they took advantage of our weaknesses.

In Thomson and Lillee they possessed the best combination of fast bowlers any captain could wish for, and our batsmen, especially early in the innings, were constantly under pressure. None of them had ever encountered bowling of such speed before and, except for Fredericks and myself, none had been to Australia before.

Throughout the series, we only had one opening stand of more than 50 and that was in the Test we won at Perth, in itself a little ironic. Gordon Greenidge was badly out of form for the entire tour and had lost his confidence, so we decided to replace him. The initial feeling among the selectors was that Baichan, the third opener, was not the man for the job; even though he had done pretty well in the state matches he had not looked happy against the pace. A lot of names were bandied around and it was decided that Rowe, who, after all, had made a lot of runs in that position against England, would be used. We then had a re-think on the matter after the first day's play and decided that Lawrence was a key man at number 3. In the end we took a real gamble and used Bernard Julien who had never opened in his life. It was a little unorthodox to say the least but Julien applied himself well to the job. Unfortunately, when we used him again in the fourth Test in Sydney, Thomson cracked his thumb and put him out for the rest of the series.

With the benefit of hindsight, we should have persevered with Greenidge – just as we did with Richards who, in the end, was elevated to the opening spot as Fredericks's partner and began his string of big scores which have been so consistent ever since. Greenidge, in addition, was a fine slip fielder and might have found himself, given the chance.

So, with this problem at the start of the innings, our key batsmen in the middle of the order were frequently coming to the crease with Thomson and Lillee fresh, their tails up and the ball relatively new. The fact that many were hit simply added to the pressure. I got struck on the jaw by Lillee in Perth and by Thomson in Sydney. As mentioned, Julien's thumb was broken, Kallicharran's nose was cracked by Lillee in Perth and, if no one else received any actual broken bones, everyone at some stage did feel the pain of a cricket ball thudding into their bodies at ninety miles an hour.

It takes a lot of courage to withstand that persistent threat of physical danger and, with six Tests packed into the tour, the problem was magnified. We finished the first Test on 2 December and were starting the second on 12 December. The third finished on 30 December and the fourth began four days later. The fifth ended on 28 January and the sixth started on 31 January. It was a heavy schedule and, if I have anything to do with it in future, I would strongly advise against the West Indies accepting six Tests in one series again.

In Roberts and Holding, we possessed the artillery which could reply to the bombardment we were receiving and they proved their worth in Perth. That, however, was the last time they were fully fit together. Holding pulled a muscle at Perth and missed the third Test and, even though they both played at Sydney and Adelaide, Roberts was well below his best with an ankle injury which finally forced him to miss the final Test. Even the support bowlers, Holder, Boyce and Julien were not available at important times through various injuries.

As far as our batsmen were concerned, there was the matter of hooking. It was only natural that with the opposition depending so heavily on fast bowling that bouncers would be a main weapon of attack and they were not sparingly used. It may well be a natural West Indian attitude to meet aggression with aggression, to fight fire with fire, and our players seemed to decide that the hook was the appropriate counter. It is a dangerous stroke at the best of times, as I well know from my early days, but on the vast Australian grounds it is doubly so – as we discovered over and over to our cost. At the end of the series, Frank Tyson brought out a book which he entitled *The Hapless Hookers* and someone counted sixteen wickets that we lost to the shot, including three at the start of our second innings in the crucial fourth Test.

We discussed the matter repeatedly at team meetings but with no apparent effect. In the end, some were pleading that they were 'compulsive hookers', whatever that meant. Surely, as professional cricketers, they should have been disciplined enough to have corrected mistakes in their play which were costing them and their team dearly?

Now to the issue of umpiring, which I have deliberately left until the last since I do not want it felt that I am whinging, as the Australians say, or complaining simply because we lost. Anyone who has played at any level knows and must accept that umpiring is an integral part of the game, that umpires are only human and that they make mistakes. In the extreme tension of Test cricket, players react angrily to what they believe is an umpiring error, but this is only natural. Generally speaking, however, there is acceptance of the principle that the umpires are in charge and that the game could not be played without them. I believe it is a principle which I personally and West Indies teams as a whole have observed.

Nevertheless, whether rightly or not we came to doubt the competence of much of the umpiring in that series, most particularly in the third Test at Melbourne.

It was a most important game with things even at one victory each after Brisbane and Perth. We batted badly after we had been sent in and only managed 224 in our first innings, which meant that a lot depended on our bowlers to get us back in the game. They did a magnificent job and we would have restricted Australia to something similar to our 224 but for a string of verdicts by the umpires which, to put it mildly, astounded us.

Redpath made 102 and it was plain to us that he was caught off his glove twice relatively early in his innings, once by Deryck Murray behind the wicket and once at legslip. Gary Cosier, playing his first Test, top-scored with 105 but, when he was 5, he got the better of an l.b.w. decision against Julien. He could not have been more *out*, to an in-swinger which caught him on the back foot right in front of the middle stump. I would say there were no fewer than seven or eight blatant mistakes, to use a charitable expression, by the umpires in that innings.

By this time all of us were totally disillusioned. I am usually a calm sort of individual but I have never been so incensed on a cricket field in my life. Every other West Indian felt the same. Gibbs, the most experienced of us all and someone who had played in every Test-playing country and was on his third tour of Australia, could take it no longer when late in the innings he had an l.b.w. appeal against Thomson refused. He angrily snatched his hat away from the umpire and, rather than give it back to him to hold the following over, stuffed it in his back pocket. It was an unusual show of petulance but it was born out of sheer frustration.

I was faced with a choice then, whether to keep quiet about the matter or whether to speak out. I opted for the latter course, although our manager, Esmond Kentish, advised against it. My attitude was that my taking such a step would highlight the problem. It certainly caused quite a stir at the time and was followed by the resignation of one of the umpires, Jack Collins of Melbourne. It was an unfortunate sequel but I had then, and still have now, no regrets at my action.

It is all well and good for those who were not in the middle or who were not part of the team to sit back and say that we should have forgotten the umpiring and got on with the game. It is not that easy and, for me at least, it was better to get it off my chest.

The most celebrated umpiring incident of the series occurred not in that third Test but in the fourth which followed at Sydney. Ironically, the overall standard of umpiring in that match was acceptable.

We had again batted first and had scored a respectable 355. We had a couple of early Australian wickets under our belt when Ian Chappell snicked the first ball he faced from Holding to Deryck Murray. It was a tremendous break-through – or so we thought. Somehow, umpire Reg Ledgwidge refused our appeal – or should I say appeals since some of us asked a second time when we did not see any immediate reaction from him. It was, to put it bluntly, a shocking decision and Holding, a quiet, soft-spoken young man off the field but an intense competitor on it, could not hide his distress. He slumped to his haunches and sobbed with anger. It took some time before he could be persuaded to bowl again and some time before he could get back into his stride. At that stage, none of us doubted that the umpiring was against us and, as we subsequently lost that Test to go 3–1 down in the series, our morale simply went to pieces. For the last month or so of the trip most of the players were simply going through the motions. They just wanted to go home.

Other things did not help the mood. Bobby Simpson had been appointed our agent before the tour started and had secured some advertising contracts for the team as a whole. It was an arrangement which brought in welcome additional revenue and it was the sort of extra-curricular activity which was to become commonplace in the near future. Yet, after a while, the obligations, such as making commercials and appearances for companies such as Brut, Shell and Ford, became a burden for players who were already fed up with the tour as a whole.

Naturally, I received a great deal of criticism for allowing the collapse of our spirit. The captain, as always, is the one everyone points the finger at when anything goes wrong yet, throughout the history of the game, even the great skippers have found it impossible to check their teams' downward slide when the tide has begun to flow against them. Try as much as I could, I found it impossible to motivate the players during those final weeks when we lost the last three Tests.

The only bright spot in that time was the form of Richards who, promoted to open, at last proved he was a great player in the making with a century at Adelaide and scores of 50 and 98 at Melbourne.

That and Lance Gibbs's feat in his final Test of surpassing Freddie Trueman's record haul of 307 wickets were only small consolations for us. We had disappointed our supporters who lost no time in letting us know when we returned home and, while it was hardly any comfort to them, we hoped they would realize that no one was more disappointed at the outcome than the players themselves.

Nevertheless, I believe that our experiences in Australia that season did serve one useful purpose. It demonstrated to the younger players who were to form the nucleus of our teams for the next few years how tough and demanding Test cricket can be. It was the first tour of Australia for Richards, Roberts, Greenidge, Holding and one or two others, and the first time they had tasted the bitterness of defeat. It might have been difficult to take at the time but it did prepare them for the arduous assignments which lay ahead.

9   Back at the Top

It is no use crying over spilt milk, I have always been told, and while the Australian defeat was a blow to the morale of us all, we had to forget it quickly. While everyone was tired and frustrated after the long, hard tour of Australia, fortunately there followed almost immediately a series at home against India and then one away against England. These got the team back into the swing of Test cricket quickly and presented an opportunity for us to pick ourselves up off the floor and prove to everyone that what happened in Australia was not a true indication of our ability.

We started the first Test against India in Barbados less than five weeks after finishing our last against Australia in Melbourne. I thought it was essential that we did not panic in our selection and drop players left and right simply because of what happened in Australia. The Indians brought very much the same team which had given us such a close run in India in the 1974–5 season and I knew they would be far stronger than most West Indians seemed to anticipate.

Somehow, there had always been a tendency in the West Indies to underestimate the Indians, even after their triumph in 1971, and this was encouraged when we won the first Test by an innings and 97 runs. It was a question of bad batting in both their innings and our batsmen making use of the excellent conditions at Kensington. At the Queen's Park Oval in Trinidad, however, the situation would be far different.

The Oval, it seems, holds a jinx for West Indian teams. In my experiences we had never gone through a series without losing at least one Test there. It was there against England in 1968 that Sobers's declaration let England in for victory and, after that, we were beaten in Trinidad by India in 1971, by Australia in 1973 and by England in the final Test in 1974. The problem concerns the pitch which is slow and does not allow for our natural stroke-play. Runs have to be grafted with concentration doubly important.

On this occasion, it was ideally suited to the Indians. Their leading batsmen, particularly Gavaskar, Viswanath and

Mohinder Amarnath, were accustomed to batting in similar conditions in India, and their great quartet of spinners, Bedi, Chandrasekhar, Prasanna and Venkataraghavan, delighted in the turn they could extract from the pitch.

For our batsmen, who had just returned from three months on the fast, bouncy pitches of Australia, batting against quick bowling almost all the time, the adjustment to an attack based on spin was difficult, while we simply did not have spinners with the experience or class to exploit the Trinidad pitch.

We had taken the decision, after Australia, to leave out Lance Gibbs, signalling the end of his great career. It was not an easy choice to make but the time had come to prepare someone else for the position which he had held for so long. He had given great service to West Indian cricket but his powers had definitely declined and he was not collecting wickets as readily as he used to. Having said that, let me add that we would probably have won the third Test – and not lost it as we did – had Lance been in the team.

As it was, we only just managed to save the second, a dropped catch from my bat when we were struggling on the final day helping us to claim a draw. We all breathed a sigh of relief that the Trinidad Test was out of the way for we knew that it was the only ground on which the Indians would have a chance. Imagine our dismay, therefore, when heavy rain forced the West Indies Board to switch the third Test from Guyana back to the Queen's Park Oval. There was disappointment for me in another respect since it would have been my first opportunity to captain a West Indies team in my native land. That, however, would have to wait for some time yet.

The old Queen's Park jinx ran true to form again, and we lost an amazing match by six wickets after leading by 131 on first innings. Holding bowled really fast in the first innings and India were routed for 228 so that the thought of them getting over 400 to win in their second innings never crossed my mind when I declared with six wickets down. Their actual target was 406 with a day and a session remaining, a target never previously achieved in Test cricket.

By this stage of the match, with the pitch playing slower and slower, we had to depend on our spinners to bring us victory but all three, Jumadeen, Padmore and the Trinidadian leg-spinner Imtiaz Ali, were inexperienced, Padmore and Imtiaz playing their first Tests. Holding could find nothing in the pitch and, I am sorry to say, the spin trio was just not up to it. Gavaskar and Vishwanath put their heads down and batted really well for centuries and young Amarnath supported them admirably. They lost only four wickets on the way, and the fact that two of them were run out does not say much for the way we bowled. Yet, since we had decided to rest a fatigued Roberts for the final two Tests and since we had made our choice about Gibbs, we could have no complaints.

So we went on to Jamaica for the final Test which would decide the rubber. Unfortunately, the match turned into a farce, and the Indians virtually surrendered it after several of their batsmen had been injured in their first innings. Bedi, their captain, and Polly Umrigar, their manager, held a press conference on the rest day and referred to the match as a war, complaining about intimidatory bowling by Holding. This, in any case, is what I read in the press. Neither of them made any comment to me about it during the match, and there was nothing said by the umpires, the two most experienced in the West Indies, Ralph Gosein and Douglas Sang Hue, either.

The Indians declared their first innings with six wickets down because, they said, they were fearful their bowlers would have been injured and batted five men short in their second innings. I must say I felt a little sorry for them at the time, but there was certainly no deliberate policy on our part to indulge in unfair tactics.

Perhaps I had better put the record straight. In the pitch at the northern end there was a particular spot from which the ball would either fly dangerously or shoot. All those batsmen hit suffered their injuries at that end. Gaekwad and Viswanath were struck by Holding, Patel by Holder but in many cases the blame lay with the Indians themselves since they frequently backed away and took their eyes off the ball. A lot was made of the fact that Holding bowled around the wicket which, according to the Indians, he did to aim at their bodies. His ploy, quite simply, was to change his direction against batsmen who were not getting into line, looking for catches behind the wicket or in the slips.

No team enjoys the sight of opponents being injured and taken off to hospital, even though it is part of the game, and the Indians unfairly blamed us for their own deficiencies and attempted to decry our win.

Not that I was greatly upset. One series was over and another one was about to start to which we had to pay our immediate attention. We left Jamaica right after that final Test against India and headed for England for a full tour, the first the West Indies were to make since 1966. I was satisfied by now that our players had put the memory of Australia behind them and knew that we had the potential to retain the Frank Worrell Trophy.

We had depth in batting and a number of outstanding fast bowlers, supplemented by the inclusion of the 21-year-old Wayne Daniel for the first time. He had played for Middlesex the previous season and made his Test debut against India in the final Test. Although he was really raw, had trouble with his run-up and bowled several wides and no-balls, he had speed and it was obvious he could be put right. Along with Roberts, Holding, Holder and Julien he would form our shock attack. We included only two spinners, Padmore, the 'offie', and Jumadeen, orthodox left-arm, mainly because there was a dearth of them at the time in West Indian cricket.

As had been the case for some years, the majority of the team had played county cricket, which was a decided advantage. We were all confident that we would do well; if we needed something to stiffen our determination, England's captain, Tony Greig, unwittingly supplied it just before the series began.

Speaking in a television interview, he said our strength had been overestimated and claimed that we were not fighters when the chips were down. He would, he said, make us 'grovel'. The word was given wide publicity in the papers and was to be a millstone around Greig's neck for the rest of the summer.

Whether Greig realized it or not, the world 'grovel' is one guaranteed to raise the blood pressure of any black man. It conjures up hated images of hundreds of years of slavery and servility, and its use was compounded, in this case, by the fact that Greig was a white South African. We were angry and West Indians everywhere were angry. We resolved to show him and everyone else that the days for grovelling were over: West Indian cricketers possessed far more character than he gave us credit for.

Every time Greig came to the wicket in that series, our fast bowlers seemed to gain an extra few miles an hour from somewhere. I will never forget Roberts charging in to the tall England skipper in the first Test at Trent Bridge and sending the off-stump reeling several yards before he had a chance to put his bat down. It was one of the fastest deliveries I have ever seen. Naturally, we had respect for Greig as a cricketer and realized he was a key batsman but it was his taunt that he would make us 'grovel' that committed our bowlers to regard him as Public Enemy Number 1.

It was a summer of blue, cloudless skies and scorching hot temperatures which, if you believe the press, suits us. We 'like the sun on our backs' is the usual phrase. Naturally, everyone likes to feel the sun on their backs playing a game designed to be played in that type of weather but, during that summer, it led to a string of slow, ideal batting pitches which really were no good for our fast bowlers.

Old Trafford was the only exception and there, where there was a little green on the pitch the ball would at least bounce over stump height, Roberts, Holding and Daniel routed England for 71 and 126 for us to win by no fewer than 425 runs. The result broke the stalemate of two draws, and we went on to win the fourth and fifth Tests as well to record the most decisive triumph in any series against England by a West Indies team.

Fortunately for us, there were no failures as such – unless you count the ageing captain who could only manage a modest average of 32 with the bat while Richards, Fredericks and Greenidge were in roaring form at the top of the order. I'll plead that when I came in there were usually plenty of runs on the board already and I had to get on with it right away!

Our batting throughout was magnificent. Richards suddenly found the formula for big innings when we promoted him to open towards the end of the Australian tour; satisfied that he had established himself, he reverted to the number 3 position for which he is ideally suited in the series against India. He responded by scoring centuries in the first three Tests and, once we got to England, showed that, if anything, his appetite was even more insatiable.

He was so self-assured that he appeared capable of anything. I think he could even have hooked a yorker for six and no one would have been surprised. His scores were phenomenal – 232 in the first Test, 4 and 135 in the third, 66 and 38 in the fourth and 291 in the fifth, for a total of 829 at an average of 118. It was more than any other West Indian had scored in a single series and to think he missed the second Test at Lord's through illness.

Greenidge and Fredericks were not that far behind and each totalled over 500 in the five Tests. With those three at the top of the order, we rarely had to worry and we topped 400 in four innings, culminating with 687 for eight declared in the final Test at the Oval.

Greenidge had been disappointing in Australia and had not played in the West Indies against India. However, he was now returning 'home' as it were. England was where he had been brought up and learned most of his cricket, and he was more at home on slower English pitches. He batted with complete authority and saved us in our first innings at Old Trafford, when he scored 134 out of 211. He followed this with another century in the second innings and then one again in the first innings of the following Test, conclusive proof, if any were needed, that here was a batsman of true class.

Fredericks probably knew it was his last series in England, although whether it was his first or his last, he would have wanted to do well. He is one of the most dedicated cricketers I know, one who has never given less than 100 per cent effort, and I could not understand why he was not given his due in some quarters. There surely could be no doubts after that season.

The most dramatic batting I have seen in Test cricket was from Fredericks, Greenidge and Richards on the first day at Leeds when we came in for tea at 330 for two – yes, 330.

In fact, our batting was so strong that summer that when Kallicharran was forced to enter hospital for an operation on his shoulder after the third Test, we could replace him with as outstanding and experienced a player as Rowe while

King and Gomes, who both totalled over 1000 runs in that season, had to share the all-rounder's position.

With such potential, and the pitches as they were, we frequently scored plenty of runs at an astonishing rate. The first day at Leeds was phenomenal because it was a Test, but there were other times when county attacks were treated even more harshly. The most spectacular was at Swansea's St Helen's Ground when we scored 554 for four declared in eighty-four overs. It was a glorious August weekend, the pitch was perfect and Glamorgan fielded a weak bowling side, so everything was right for it.

Personally, I scored an undefeated 201 in exactly two hours which equalled the fastest time ever recorded for a first-class double-century by Gilbert Jessop way back. That really didn't matter to me at the time because, in the circumstances, it was hardly a great occasion. Yet it is nice to have your name in the record books so that when old age creeps in the new generation won't forget you quite so quickly!

If our batting produced runs in sufficient quantity and quickly enough to give us plenty of time to bowl out our opponents, the fast bowlers were the ones who turned that advantage into final victory. Holding and Roberts claimed twenty-eight wickets each, Holder fifteen and Daniel thirteen, and they were the only ones to bowl more than 100 overs. That was the extent of their domination.

Because of the dry weather, we tended at first towards balancing our attack with at least one spinner. Yet when we did include Padmore at Old Trafford he bowled only three overs and we decided then that we would depend solely on pace, partly because it was our strongest suit and we had so much of it, but principally because England's batsmen were so uncomfortable against it.

Our policy almost came unstuck in the final Test at the Oval, played on one of the slowest Test pitches I have ever experienced. The scores correctly indicated just how easy it was: West Indies 687 for eight declared, of which Richards scored his 291, and 185 for none declared; England 435, Amiss marking his return to Test cricket with a double century, and 203. I had to call on Fredericks and Richards for comparatively long spells and yearned then for a decent spinner, if only to vary things.

Fortunately, in these adverse conditions, Holding produced the finest fast bowling I have ever witnessed in Test cricket. Others might have bowled faster in a particular spell, although I even doubt that, and others might have been more dangerous because of a lively pitch. But for sustained speed and accuracy, it would be impossible to improve on Holding's performance. He claimed eight for 92 in thirty-three overs in the first innings; when England needed to bat out the final day to save the match, he followed that up with six for 57 from twenty overs. Of those fourteen victims, twelve were either bowled or leg before, irrefutable tribute to his pace and his accuracy.

England's selectors, it must be admitted, did little to help their team's cause. They brought back the veteran Brian Close for the first three Tests and used him and John Edrich to open the innings at Old Trafford. No one could ever doubt the ability and courage of the two left-handers but Close was in his mid-forties and Edrich was no spring-chicken himself. We received a lot of carping criticism when Holding and Daniel bowled them a succession of bouncers late one afternoon of their second innings at Old Trafford but, as always, I felt that the umpires were there to enforce the laws. If they were not prepared to rule that the bowling was intimidatory, I did not feel it my duty to intervene.

I was more concerned with the futility of the bowling since it was not the type of attack designed to get wickets. Edrich and Close might have been bruised a bit at the end of play but they were still together and that was not good enough as far as I was concerned. Afterwards, we had a long talk about the value of fast bowling of full length, with the bouncer as a surprise weapon. The results were evident for the rest of the tour, when far fewer bouncers were used.

Since we had depended so heavily on fast bowling for our success in England during that summer, everyone in the West Indies was naturally concerned with injuries sustained in the very first Shell Shield match of the following season rendered Holding and Daniel unfit for the series against Pakistan. The Pakistanis were touring the West Indies for the first time in nineteen years and, if nothing else, possessed an enormously powerful batting team. On our pitches we

93

would need to be at full strength to hold our own against them, especially since they were full of self-confidence after beating Australia in a short series in Australia just prior to arriving.

It was a godsend, therefore, when, almost out of the blue, two new fast bowlers emerged during that season to fill the breach left by Holding and Daniel.

One was Colin Croft, a tall, well-built Guyanese who I remembered as a very raw youngster some years earlier. The other was Joel Garner, a giant of a man at 6 feet 8 inches who Wes Hall had mentioned to me the year before as having a lot of promise. He had played club cricket with Wes in Barbados and now I was to see for myself how correct Wes's judgement was.

Both did well in early Shield matches and forced their way into the team so that we could depend, yet again, on a strong pace attack. In the end, Croft, troubling batsmen both with genuine speed and his movement off the pitch from leg, finished with thirty-three wickets, Garner with twenty-five and Roberts with nineteen and we clinched what was a very close and interesting series 2–1. That loss, inevitably, came in the second of the two Tests played at Queen's Park Oval, but since we won the first one there, the old jinx had not been completely at work.

The interest in each Test never flagged. We struggled throughout the last day to save the first at Kensington Oval in Barbados, the last two wickets holding out in the final twenty overs while the Pakistanis became more and more panicky. We then won the second in Trinidad comfortably, were held to a draw in the third in Guyana after leading by over 200 on first innings, lost on a spinner's pitch in Trinidad second time round and, finally, secured the series in Jamaica when I thought we played better, all round, than we had done for some time.

As always, I had my ups and downs that season. In the first innings of the first Test, we were faced with a Pakistan total of 435 and I helped us recover from a ticklish situation by making 157 and sharing a big stand of 151 for the sixth wicket with Deryck Murray. Having not got a big score in England the previous season, I was happy to be back with a century – and one so important to the course of the match.

After that, however, the cupboard with my runs in it seemed to have been shut fast again.

My biggest disappointment was in Guyana where I pulled a muscle after only twenty minutes of the Test and for the rest of the match, with the exception of a few minutes while I attempted to bat, had to watch from the pavilion. The previous year the weather had forced the Georgetown Test against India to be switched back to Trinidad, so my second opportunity to skipper the West Indies in my homeland had now gone.

To make matters worse, I felt we allowed that game to slip away from us when we gave away too many runs in Pakistan's second innings by setting attacking fields. The pitch was still good when they went in a second time and picked up numerous boundaries to vacant third man and fine leg positions. We should have made them fight harder for their runs but, as Deryck Murray had taken over, I felt he should be the one to make the decisions, although we did discuss tactics off the field.

The most significant off-the-field discussions during that series, as it turned out, had nothing to do with how we should check the left-handed Wasim Raja's flow of runs, or why we should bring back the veteran all-rounder David Holford for the final Test (with favourable results, I might add), or which one of the fast bowlers should open the bowling. They dealt, in fact, with nothing concerning that rubber at all but with the formation of what was to become World Series Cricket.

Some of the most momentous events in cricketing history were just around the corner, and they were to affect my life and the lives of every other cricketer and cricket follower profoundly.

10   The Packer Affair

What was to develop into one of the most furious controversies the game has ever known began for me one afternoon in April 1977 at the Queen's Park Oval in Trinidad. It was during the fourth Test against Pakistan, and Mushtaq Mohammad, the Pakistani captain, was the one who first hinted at the development.

There was, according to Mushtaq, 'something brewing' in international cricket; an Australian by the name of Austin Robertson was staying at the Port-of-Spain Hilton and wanted to talk to me. Mushtaq had obviously seen him earlier and advised that I should do the same.

I simply had no inclination as to what was up when I dined with Robertson at the Hilton that evening. I had been around Australian cricket a lot but had never heard his name so was unprepared for what he had to say. As I was to discover from him, he was part of a group, including some prominent Australian cricketers, which was planning to stage a series in Australia the following season between a selected Australian team and a world team.

It would be completely divorced from the Australian Board, Robertson said, and would have substantial financial backing from a television channel owned by a Mr Kerry Packer which would broadcast all the games.

Robertson then offered me a contract at a fee staggering in relationship to what I was earning from the game at the time. I am sure he must have noticed me almost choke over the fruit salad when the matter of finance and security was mentioned.

Robertson, young, fresh-faced and soft-spoken, put his case sincerely and precisely. He had been involved for many years with professional sport, his father had been the professional sprint champion of Australia and he himself had been an Australian Rules footballer of some note in Perth. In addition, the Packer media group in Australia was internationally known and respected and financially strong.

This was all well and good but I wanted to hear the case put by a professional cricketer. I wanted to know reason why someone like Ian Chappell had decided to participate in such

96

...erging from a lean spell at Adelaide, 1980. *Patrick Eagar*

Returning to the pavilion at Bourda with Basil Butcher after add[i] 171 for the fourth wicket in the 1967 Shell Shield match agai[n] Jamaica.

rkeley Gaskin, DCC stalwart and a fast-medium bowler for Guyana
d the West Indies chats with Conrad Hunte and David Allan as
nager of the 1963 West Indies team to England.

ght-arm over, medium-pace-seam — a style of bowling which I
eloped with Haslingden in the Lancashire League. *Patrick Eagar*

The ceremony to mark the retirement of Jackie Bond during
Warwickshire game at Old Trafford, 1974, was a moving affair.

Snow caused play to be abandoned early in 1975 for Lancashire's ga
against Derbyshire at Buxton. David Lloyd, Frank Hayes, mys
Dickie Bird and Peter Lever. *G. Hallawell* (Hallawell Photos).

anager Clyde Walcott introduces me to Her Majesty the Queen as
est Indies captain during the Lord's Test, 1976. *Daily Mirror*

great moment. Holding the Prudential World Cup and the Man of
e Match award aloft after the presentation by Prince Philip after the
75 final. *Patrick Eagar*

One of the many shots which came off the middle of the bat in the 19 World Cup Final at Lord's, hooking Dennis Lillee for six. *Patr Eagar*

The exuberant 1976 team. Michael Holding, having just bowled t England captain for the second time in the match, is surrounded jubilant team-mates Collis King, Vivian Richards, Deryck Murr Roy Fredericks and myself. *Patrick Eagar*

th Kerry Packer and Sir Gary Sobers before World Series Cricket's nch in 1977. *P.B.L.*

families Chappell and Lloyd share Christmas day in Melbourne, 7. *P.B.L.*

For me, fielding has always been a great joy — the photo of the rat[]
youthful Lloyd was taken back in 1972. Today I still manage to h[]
on to a few catches, such as that to dismiss Dennis Lillee off Bern[]
Julien at Perth in the 1975-6 series. *Patrick Eagar*

a venture. Clearly, Robertson and his associates realized this would be an important consideration for all the players they approached and he brought along a cassette tape in which Ian Chappell spoke about the scheme for almost three-quarters of an hour.

Ian Chappell is always someone I have respected as a cricketer and as a friend. Because of his forthright manner and his conviction that the players deserved better, he has had his confrontations with authority. He has been misunderstood by many people who mistakenly see him as a renegade but it is significant that, among the cricketers I know, he enjoys almost unanimous esteem.

On the tape Chappell outlined the background to the development. He explained how he felt that interest in cricket was increasing but that not enough effort was being made to exploit its true potential. The envisaged series, involving as it would some of the best players in the world and guaranteed wide television coverage, was bound to be a success, he argued. In addition, the players would now be paid what they were truly worth. And he stressed that it would be no fly-by-night operation. It would be arranged and financially supported by one of the largest organizations in Australia.

It sounded good, but there were plenty of questions that I had to answer in my own mind first. Fortunately, my wife, Waveney, was in Trinidad at the time so we were able to discuss it at length. Robertson wanted an immediate answer and the lawyer who accompanied him, John Kitto, explained much of the legal jargon in the contract. However, there was no way I was going to rush into such an undertaking without careful study and it was two days before I finally signed on the dotted line.

Several factors swayed me, principally the financial security which the contract offered. I would be paid Aus.$30,000 a season with all expenses provided, a figure most cricketers never imagined possible, compared with the less than one-third of that figure which I had received for skippering the West Indies in England in 1976.

I had seen the plight of many great West Indian players of the past following their exit from the game and it was not particularly comforting. Several had been forced to continue

97

playing in the Leagues of England while Caribbean governments had created coaching posts for others. I did not see myself following either course, and here now was an opportunity to earn and invest the kind of money which would allow me to be confident of my future after my playing days were over.

Naturally, there was the West Indian captaincy to consider. It is a responsible position and one which I do not regard lightly, yet I realized that I would have to relinquish it should I accept the contract which Robertson had placed before me.

Yet I did not feel that, by signing, I was leaving West Indian cricket in the lurch or betraying it in any way. I have given the best years of my life in its cause, had suffered many heartaches and insults and, as captain, had helped mould a strong, young side. As I saw it, my own career had another three years at the most to run and whoever took over the captaincy would have the nucleus of an excellent team at his disposal.

Having signed, I learned that Andy Roberts and Vivian Richards had also accepted offers to participate in the world team while Michael Holding, who was injured at the time and was in Jamaica, was worried only over the South African question. He wished to be assured that he would not be obliged to play there and, after receiving the assurance, agreed to join. As far as I was concerned, I knew that there was no way I could be forced to play in South Africa against my better judgement, contract or no contract, and, even though there would be South Africans in the world side, they would be those engaged with English counties against whom we played regularly in any case.

So the die was cast.

Although we were asked to keep the details of the agreement to ourselves, since any 'leak' could scuttle the entire exercise, it would be impossible – and, in my estimation, unjust – not to discuss it with Deryck Murray, as Secretary of the West Indies Players Association, and not to inform the President of the West Indies Cricket Board of Control, Jeffrey Stollmeyer, of the proposal.

It was Deryck, in fact, who mentioned it to Stollmeyer, whose initial reaction was most understanding. His only concern was that we should be careful over the South African connection, an extremely delicate issue which could have serious repercussions. Later, he was to state that he could not see how anyone could have any quarrel with players for wanting to do as well as they could financially, especially since the length of their playing careers was limited.

Tony Greig, who was to captain the world team, also arrived in Port-of-Spain around the same time with his wife, on the pretext of having a busman's holiday while signing up Imran Khan, the Pakistani fast bowler, for Sussex. In fact, he was there to influence those Pakistanis he wanted to join his team and, when I met with him at the Hilton, he was most enthusiastic about the new venture.

As far as I was concerned, that was the end of it and I would be travelling to Australia later in the year as part of a world team under Greig. However, new situations were to develop fast and furiously.

Details of the series were revealed by the press in England sometime in May and the reaction was instant. 'Pirates' and 'rebels' were words widely used to describe 'Packer cricket' and those who had signed for it. The International Cricket Conference met with Kerry Packer at Lord's to see if any arrangement could be reached by which there would be no clash with Test cricket, but that meeting broke down. The ICC then decided to ban all those who had signed for World Series Cricket, as it was to be known, and then followed the celebrated court case which Kerry Packer won on every count.

Instead of getting weaker in the face of opposition, World Series Cricket became stronger. Austin Robertson called me from Australia and asked if I would choose a full West Indian touring party of sixteen to form one of the teams for an extended series. Every day the press would announce the names of new Australians or world players who had been added to the ever-growing list.

Of the squad which I handed to Robertson, all accepted the contracts offered with the exception of Alvin Kallicharran, which was fair enough. The others appeared to have no qualms about joining WSC, but it was an individual decision each man had to make for himself and I certainly held nothing against Kalli for going the way he felt was best for him.

By now, I had become very much involved in the exercise. There would be repeated telephone calls at odd hours from Australia on a variety of subjects concerning the West Indian squad; I had a meeting with John Cornell, one of the WSC executives from Australia, during the Test at Old Trafford between England and Australia and spoke with Dennis Lillee in Australia to hear his views.

My main interest, however, was in meeting the man who was the central figure in what had become a raging controversy. Knowing that Kerry Packer was in London, I requested a meeting with him. He provided the return airline ticket from Manchester to London, despatched a limousine, complete with liveried driver, to pick me up at Heathrow and deliver me, as it were, to his suite at the Dorchester.

With such lavish treatment and with the adverse publicity he was receiving in the British press, I full expected to meet a flash businessman, somewhat direct in his dealings, completely ignorant of cricket but expert in the area of dollars and cents.

Instead, I found Kerry Packer, at our very first meeting, to be natural and down-to-earth with a genuine interest in all sports and a knowledge of cricket far greater than he had been given credit for. Naturally, he was tough and he talked strongly about his encounters with the 'establishment', both in Australia and in England. But I felt at ease in his company and we struck up an excellent relationship. Subsequently, we have spoken on many subjects and seldom has he struck me as talking about anything but sound common sense, whether the subject be Viv Richards's batting, race relations or politics.

Unfortunately, I didn't have the same affinity with certain other individuals that particular summer. It happened to be my benefit year and, for some reason not clear to me, I was told support was affected by my affiliation to Packer and World Series Cricket. I would like to disprove that theory and think, instead, that injury which necessitated knee operations for the removal of cartilages and which limited my appearances were responsible for the diminishing returns to the benefit fund.

Lancashire had been wonderful to me over the years, and in return, I believe I had always tried my best for them. The people had been tremendous and I considered myself an integral part of Old Trafford. It was hurtful, therefore, to observe the change in attitudes amongst so many members when it was learned I would be part of World Series Cricket, particularly since my actions were in no way going to affect my appearances for Lancashire in the future.

By the end of summer, details of the Australian adventure were known. The West Indies team had been finalized, after a frantic search party for Jim Allen, a replacement for Kallicharran, located him in a League team somewhere in Wales. There would be night games under lights, pitches were being artificially prepared in hot houses, and teams would wear coloured clothing. The British press, with its fleet of reactionary cricket correspondents, immediately dubbed the whole exercise a 'circus'.

I knew better. Kallicharran apart, we had the best team we could assemble, the Australians were also as strong as they probably could be and the World team was an exciting combination. Whether the ball was white or red and whether the outfit was cream or coloured, the best cricketers in the world would provide the best cricket. I was determined it would be no circus for our team since the memories of the 1975-6 defeat were still painfully recent.

Our squad was: C.H. Lloyd (captain), D.L. Murray (vice-captain), C.G. Greenidge, R.C. Fredericks, I.V.A. Richards, L.G. Rowe, J.C. Allen, C.L. King, D.A.J. Holford, B.D. Julien, A.M.E. Roberts, M.A. Holding, J. Garner, W.W. Daniel, A.L. Padmore. In other words, we had nine of the eleven who had played the previous Test for the West Indies against Pakistan, the exceptions being Kallicharran and Colin Croft.

Mainly on the suggestion of Tony Greig Dr Rudi Webster, a Barbadian specialist living in Melbourne, was appointed as our manager. At first, Bill Jacobs, who managed the world team in 1971-2 in Australia, was recommended for the post but Rudi, a former first-class player for Scotland and Warwickshire, was a West Indian and knew, and was known by, most of the players. In his two seasons with us, he did a tremendous job.

As far as we were concerned – and as far as the West Indian public was concerned – we were representing the West Indies against Australia, and the contest was every bit as tense and demanding as a Test match. We were to play three Supertests against Australia for the Sir Garfield Sobers Trophy and we were intent that Gary should present it to us when the series was over.

Well, we not only won the Sobers Trophy by defeating Australia 2–1 in the Supertests, but we also took the International Cup limited-overs competition and claimed Aus.$77,475 of the prize money that was being offered. The brilliant batting of Richards and our strong fast bowling were the features of our cricket. In addition, no team in my experience has ever caught and fielded as we did that season. We did not miss a thing in the slips and the ball was flying in that direction pretty often. The ground work was equally outstanding and there was not a weak arm in the team.

It is true that the Australians were not quite the force they had been two seasons earlier, especially since Jeff Thomson had opted out after initially signing for WSC, but I believe that the way we played would have beaten even that side at its best.

For most followers of the game, however, the results were immaterial. The main issue was whether the venture would succeed. Would the crowds accept it? Would the artificial pitches be up to standard. Would top-class cricket be possible under lights? How about the white ball. In short, would Packer make it?

Initially, the crowds were so poor that it was only natural we should all be somewhat apprehensive about the success of the undertaking. There had been an extensive promotional campaign, the most imaginative I had ever seen for cricket anywhere with advertisements on television, radio and posters, special appearances by the players and the like – yet there were only about 2000 spectators for each day of the first Supertest at VFL Park in Melbourne.

VFL Park is a vast concrete stadium, built to accommodate up to 80,000 spectators for football matches. It was never designed for cricket, and even less so for 2000 cricket spectators. There was absolutely no atmosphere and, to those who had played before crowds of 80,000 at the Melbourne

Cricket Ground in Test cricket only two seasons earlier, it was somewhat depressing.

Yet all of us knew what it was to play to vast, empty seats. Most of us had played county cricket in England, where many times during a season it was almost impossible to count the number of diehards watching on the fingers of one hand. Personally, I knew that interest would increase as long as we played good cricket, since it was on television and the television coverage was the best to be seen anywhere.

The press is a powerful media and it certainly proved its strength in painting an image in the public's mind that, somehow, World Series Cricket was not the real thing, that it was a 'circus'. The Australian Cricket Board, staging their series against India simultaneously, recognized its chance to promote the Tests as 'fair-dinkum cricket', and it was some time before we could overcome the skilful propaganda mounted against us.

Yet the barrier was gradually broken. Midway through the season, crowds began to creep up over the five-figure mark, particularly for the International Cup matches, and Australians came to accept that the cricket was of a high standard and that the contests were every bit as competitive as Test cricket. Just after Christmas, Waveney, who had joined me with the two girls in Australia, had to enter hospital for a back operation. Visiting her, I knew from the favourable comments of doctors and nurses that we were making the breakthrough; WSC was overcoming the obstacles which had been placed in its way by those who had a vested interest in seeing it fail.

None of us were under any illusions about the criticism and, quite regularly, the downright abuse which would be hurled at us. We had experienced the reaction in England and could not expect things to be far different in Australia. However, we had to ignore it all and simply perform to the best of our ability.

We were all lifted by the way we were treated and by the competence of the organization.

WSC assisted with passages and accommodation so that several wives and families were able to join their cricketing husbands, a gesture never afforded in my eleven years of cricket with the West Indies and much appreciated by all concerned, particularly over the Christmas and New Year period. Special areas were set aside at all the grounds for guests of players to watch the cricket in comfort, a nursery even being provided so that wives would not have the bother of worrying about baby-sitters.

The standard of the hotels at which we stayed was uniformly high, and WSC provided an office in each to which we could carry any queries or problems. Everything, from a game of squash to a trip around Sydney Harbour, could be arranged by the office.

We were royally treated and I think we all responded accordingly on the field.

In addition, all the teams stayed at the same hotels, engendering a feeling of camaraderie I had never previously experienced in international cricket. A sense of unity prevailed, also assisted, no doubt, by the nature of the exercise and a certain pioneer spirit. It was commonplace to have breakfast with one of the Australian or world team boys or to enter the hotel bar to find it packed with players from different countries, of different races and religions, having a drink together or, on one or two cases, vying for the attention of some particularly attractive young Australian lass!

The Christmas Day party in 1977, put on by WSC at the Old Melbourne Inn, proved an unforgettable event. All players and officials attended, with Eddie Barlow dressed as Santa Claus to present gifts to all the children; the food was magnificent; the wine and the rum punch flowed; and to top it off, we even had a limbo-dancing competition between Collis King and Tony Greig!

Of all the innovations during the first season, night cricket proved the most spectacularly successful. All doubts about whether the lighting would be adequate, whether the white ball would be acceptable and so on were dispelled. The twilight period proved a little difficult for sighting the ball, and it did become somewhat tarnished towards the end of forty eight-ball overs, but these were hardly serious handicaps.

Night cricket was ideal for spectators, almost 25,000 of whom came out for the second match of the season between Australia and the West Indies to witness a remarkable finish.

We needed 6 to win with two balls to go and Garner and Daniel at the wicket. The tension among our players was as great as I have known it and when Daniel, somehow, managed to hit Malone into the crowd at long-on for six off the seventh ball of the final over, sheer pandemonium broke loose. I wish those critics who suggested that WSC cricket didn't mean much to the players could have witnessed the scenes that night.

Not that it would have mattered, I suppose. The campaign was to nail Packer cricket and the truth did not seem to count. Several correspondents, including those from England, suggested that we had instructed bowlers not to bowl bouncers in night cricket. It was quite true that hardly any bouncers were bowled but they conveniently omitted from their assessment the fact that umpires call wides for bouncers in the limited-over game and this was the reason why there were so few about. In fact, I cannot recall very many being bowled in the various one-day competitions in England for that very reason – but, because it was WSC, some devious motive had to be found.

The critics were proved wrong too in the matter of the pitches. Since every first-class ground was made unavailable, WSC had to turn to the unlikeliest of places to stage its matches. Football parks in Melbourne and Adelaide where the hot-house, pre-prepared pitches were laid, a trotting stadium in Perth (Gloucester Park), and the Sydney Showground, venue for pop concerts, speedway racing, horse shows and agricultural exhibitions, but never for cricket. It was reasonable to assume that conditions would be difficult, yet John Maley, the conscientious curator, proved a real magician.

The artificial pitches at both venues were low and slow but no worse than many on which I have played Tests, while those in Perth and Sydney, particularly the latter, were tremendous. It was the consensus among the players, in fact, that the Showground pitch was the best in Australia – hard, fast and true.

Not all the innovations met with the players' approval. The main complaint was the distance to be travelled from the hotel in Melbourne to VFL Park, some seventeen miles away, a journey that would take forty-five minutes to an hour in the coach, and the late finishes to the night matches. One night match, in fact, did not end until after midnight which meant arriving back at the hotel at around 2 a.m. – then being ready to leave at 11 next morning for another night match.

What with constant travelling from city to city, demands on players for promotional appearances and coaching sessions and the absence of any of the usual state matches to have a breather, it was an exacting schedule. Granted, we were being paid handsomely for our services but I could not help but feel that performances on the field could be affected and, after all, it is through our performances on the field that we are judged.

11   The Split with the Board

World Series Cricket's first season ended in Melbourne on 12 February, and we turned our attention to the Test series against Australia in the West Indies which was just around the corner.

WSC did clash with two Test series during the first year – Australia against India at home and England against Pakistan in Pakistan. An effort to have the WSC Pakistanis included in their team against England came to nothing; England were missing the services of Greig, Knott, Underwood, Amiss and Woolmer; and the Australians were making do with a very young and inexperienced team under the captaincy of the veteran Bobby Simpson, recalled in his country's hour of need, after ten years away from the Test scene.

As far as the West Indies were concerned, however, there was no such problem. All of us who were with the WSC were free for the series against Australia and, when asked whether we would be available, only Roy Fredericks and David Holford indicated that they would not be. Although I pleaded with him to change his mind, Freddo said he would retire from Test cricket to concentrate his attention on World Series. He was playing too much, he said, and his three-year contract with WSC would suffice. David, by this time almost 38, said he had had enough and doubted whether he would be picked again anyhow.

The West Indies Board had been inconsistent in its attitude to WSC and those players who signed. After Jeff Stollmeyer's early statement that he could not blame cricketers for wanting to maximize their earnings, the Board's representatives (Stollmeyer and his former Test opening partner Allan Rae) had gone along with the ICC vote to ban all WSC players from Test cricket. Yet they contended that they were against the move in principle and had only acceded for the sake of unity.

The first international against the Australians – who picked none of their WSC men for the tour and who were again under Simpson's captaincy – was a one-day match in Antigua on 22 February. Since Waveney was still recovering from the back operation she had received in Australia, I wanted to remain in Manchester for a time to ensure that she had settled in and would be well looked after during the recuperation period. So I asked the Board's permission to miss that game and return in time for the first Test, which was readily granted.

When I eventually arrived in Port-of-Spain to prepare for the first Test, I could sense that the dispute over WSC, which had been so acrimonious in England and Australia, was also simmering in the West Indies. The feeling was less intense and, as far as the public was concerned, there was widespread support for the concept. Everywhere we went, people would ask about cricket under the lights, the artificial pitches and so on, and tell us how good it was that we were now earning what we deserved.

Nevertheless, there was a definite coolness on the part of some officials – and I do not believe this was my suspicious imagination running riot. Deryck Murray, captain in my place for the one-day international, told me how he was never consulted in the selection of the team for that match and had simply been handed the team list on a piece of paper, even down to the twelfth man. Before the first Test started, Deryck and I met with the Board to negotiate fees on behalf of the Players' Association, which was standard operating procedure, since we had had no opportunity to do it before. At that meeting, attended by Jeffrey Stollmeyer, as Board President, Harold Burnett, as Secretary and Dick Hobday, as Treasurer, both myself and Deryck sensed an intolerance never previously evident.

There was no problem with the selection for the first Test team, although I was flabbergasted when Joey Carew, the new chairman of the panel, came to me in the dressing room just before the scheduled start on the first day to inform me that Vivian Richards had been appointed vice-captain instead of Deryck Murray. As one of the selectors, I should have been consulted on the move, and I knew that Clyde Walcott had returned to Barbados so was unlikely to have been consulted either. However, Carew said the other selectors had agreed and that was it.

I could see no valid reason for the change but that was not the point. If the other selectors wanted it that way, all well and good, but surely the captain should have been part of that decision and should have been able to put his views. In addition, it was hardly any way to break the news, just before the start of a Test.

We had no difficulty in winning the first two Tests at the Queen's Park Oval in Trinidad and at Kensington Oval in Barbados. Our three fast bowlers, Roberts, Croft and Garner, aided by the off-spin of Parry who impressed in his very first series, proved too much for the inexperienced Australian batsmen.

Of our batsmen, Kallicharran scored a vital century in Trinidad, which has always been a happy hunting ground for him; together we added 170 for the fourth wicket which, just about settled the issue after Australia had been bowled out for 90 on a slightly damp pitch on the first day.

In Barbados we also won comfortably, in three days as in Trinidad and by ten wickets. Yet it was a much better contest than it might appear, and it took a gritty innings of 60 by Deryck Murray to put us right in our first innings after Jeff Thomson demonstrated to West Indians the type of fury which we had experienced first hand in Australia in 1975-6.

He had not bowled flat out in Trinidad, probably because of the nature of the pitch, but in the last session of the first day in Barbados, he worked up real fire and dismissed Greenidge, Richards and Kallicharran. The Bajan crowd was humming at the end of it for they know their cricket and, of course, had produced so many great fast bowlers themselves. Luckily for us, Thomson seemed to have spent himself with that effort and he was nothing like as fearsome for the rest of the match. Still, people were able to see what we had to contend with in Australia – and Lillee was not even at the other end!

So, after two Tests, we were two up. Perhaps we were not playing against the best Australian team but it was, nevertheless, a team which had just completed a victory in a series against India and it was Test cricket. The players were pleased and, judging by their size and their reaction, so were the crowds. Everyone now looked forward to the third Test in Georgetown.

By this time, there had been a number of pertinent developments, all of which were to combine to have far-reaching effects.

During the Barbados Test, Austin Robertson arrived from Australia to recruit new, young players from the West Indies squad for World Series Cricket. We had had only fifteen in our party for the first season and, with the heavy itinerary, needed more. He approached Haynes, a dashing young opening batsman who had captured everyone's imagination with his three half-centuries in the two Tests, Croft, the fast bowler, and Austin, the all-rounder who was an excellent utility player able to do almost anything.

The position was outlined to them by Robertson, and they were given time to think it over and take their particular course. Croft, I know, was cautious at first and sought advice from Clyde Walcott on the matter. I daresay Haynes and Austin also consulted trusted advisers before making up their minds – the proper thing to do.

By the end of the Test, all three had decided to join WSC. Apparently, the Board had earlier spoken to them casually about the possibility of a long-term contract for the scheduled tour to India later in the year, but they had heard nothing further and now saw the opportunity of playing in Australia for the first time for excellent fees.

The Board reacted angrily, issuing a statement which claimed they had 'given a verbal undertaking' that they wouldn't sign any contract until the Board came up with one, supposedly just before the third Test. It spoke of a 'breach of trust' by the players, a naïve view since I could not understand why their own contract had to wait until after the second Test.

By this time, Deryck Murray, as Secretary of the Players' Association, had received a letter from the Board asking him to indicate by 23 March whether the WSC-contracted players would be available for the tour to India. This was a most unusual request, we felt, something that had never arisen before and referring, as it did, only to WSC players.

Yet we contacted WSC in Australia, explaining the position, and were told that WSC was hoping to arrange a meeting with the Indian Board for early April to try to regularize the dates of the tour so that the WSC season would not clash with it. Consequently, we asked the Board for a deferment of its 23 March deadline.

During that series, I was providing a weekly column for the *Truth* newspaper in Australia through Alan Shiell, a former South Australian state player and now a journalist covering the series for several Australian papers. When he came to my room at the Caribbee Hotel just after the Barbados Test to take notes for the *Truth* column, he told me that he had got it from 'a Board source' that the West Indies team would be changed after the third Test in Guyana. This came as news to me and, since I was one of the selectors and nothing of the sort had ever been hinted at our meetings, I dismissed it as pure rumour and conjecture.

It was not very long before I realized that there was plenty of substance to Alan Shiell's assertion. The team for the third Test was to be picked at the Pegasus Hotel in Georgetown on Easter Sunday and all the selectors – Carew, Clyde Walcott, J.K. Holt and myself – had assembled as usual. I must admit that I was unprepared for anything drastic. As I saw it, we should retain the winning combination which had brought us such resounding victories in Trinidad and Barbados since there had been no failures as such and the team was so well balanced.

The first hint I had that something was in the air was in the hotel lobby even before the meeting began. A friend of mine was waiting for me and, when I told him I had an appointment to select the Test team, he asked if he should wait. Usually, such meetings take an hour, an hour and a half at the most and he, like myself, could see no problems in choosing an eleven which had just won two Tests inside three days. Yet Joey Carew, who was close by, advised my friend not to wait, as it would probably be a long session.

No sooner had the discussion begun than it was obvious my three co-selectors had held their own meeting before and had mapped out strategy. There was talk about the future and about the possible unavailability of the WSC players for the tour of India. It would be best to bring in a few players who would certainly be available for India to give them Test experience.

That, I contended, was nonsense. They were making judgements on pure speculation which, in the end, might turn out to be completely incorrect. Our job was to pick the best team available for the particular match. If they wanted to blood young players at all, this possibly could be done once we had secured the series but to do so now would jeopardize our chances. Personally, I could see no reason to change, and I stuck by that because the other selectors could provide no valid reasons for making the alterations they wanted.

Several times during that meeting, I boiled over with anger since I could not get the others to see what I regarded to be a right and principled point of view. Once J.K. Holt interjected: 'Wait, do you mean to say we can't drop anybody now?' It was a silly comment but I replied just the same: 'Not without justification.'

We sat down at about 9 p.m. and by 2 a.m., when I found I had got nowhere, I simply gave up trying to put my views any more. A team was eventually produced excluding Deryck Murray, a reliable player over the years who had just helped save a difficult situation for us with the bat in the Barbados Test, Haynes, and Austin, who had had little opportunity yet to prove himself. David Murray, Larry Gomes and Basil Williams were to take their places.

There was no way I was going to be associated with this selection and I refused to add my signature to the list which the others had agreed to.

I knew, there and then, that I could not continue as captain but I needed to think it over first when I had time to myself. On leaving the Pegasus, I went home but the more I thought about it, the more my conviction became stronger. Within an hour, I telephoned Joey Carew to inform him that I was resigning the captaincy and withdrawing from the team which had been chosen. He asked me to reconsider and said something like: 'Oh, you'll feel differently in the morning.' I told him it was morning already and my decision, not hastily taken, was final.

I then called Deryck Murray who had remained over for a few days at the Caribbee Hotel in Barbados to tell him what had transpired. It was, by now, about 3 a.m. and Deryck was roused from a deep slumber by the telephone, yet he was coherent enough to assure me that he believed I was right in my actions and that he was certain the other players would feel the same way. Next morning, I cabled Harold Burnett, secretary of the West Indies Board, formally informing him of my decision and not long after that the WSC West Indian players announced they were also withdrawing as a vote of no confidence in the selectors.

My own position was put in a statement which I issued in Georgetown on 29 March. It read:

I have resigned as captain of the West Indies cricket team because I believe that the time has come for the West Indies Cricket Board of Control to make very clear the principles underlying the selection of the present team and to take whoever is selected as captain into their confidence in terms of the criteria for selection.

I agree completely with the principle of building a young West Indian team that will be available for playing in India but, if that is what is happening, I find it difficult to understand the dropping of young and brilliant Desmond Haynes. On the other hand, in building a young team one needs to ensure that one does not entirely turn one's back on tried and proven players and, in this context, the dropping of Deryck Murray, who was so instrumental in our winning the second Test, is incomprehensible, bearing in mind that World Series Cricket players have made themselves available for this tour and may be available for the West Indies tour of India.

However, once the basis of selection is clarified, I am willing to give my fullest support to any West Indian team chosen on clear and known principles. I believe that the present situation can be resolved by dialogue, held in private between the players and the Board and, I myself, would be available for such discussions.

It has always been for me the greatest possible honour to represent my country and my region and I look forward to being accorded the honour in future.

My agreeing to play in World Series Cricket organised by Kerry Packer has not interfered with my resolve to use my skills in the interest of my people in Guyana and in the West Indies whose help and encouragement have made me what I am. I stand ready and available to respond to any requests from any of our players for whatever help and assistance I can give.

As soon as it became known that the WSC players were out, a new team was chosen, with Kallicharran as captain. There was an airline strike on at the time affecting BWIA, the main link between Guyana and the rest of the West Indies, yet the replacement players appeared to have no trouble getting to Georgetown in what seemed a matter of hours. Two of them, Alvin Greenidge and Sylvester Clarke from Barbados, were even in Guyana already. The Board said they were on holiday but, since they had their cricket kit with them, it seemed more than just coincidence. To me, it was clear that the selectors suspected what might have happened and prepared for the eventuality.

In the meantime, all sorts of moves were taking place on the 'diplomatic front'. I had called Waveney in Manchester the morning following the selection meeting and explained the position. She appreciated my stand, as I knew she would, although I got the sneaking feeling that she was happy I would be returning home earlier than planned! Kerry Packer telephoned from Australia after the news broke there saying he was sorry about what had happened but agreeing that I was hardly left with any other choice. In addition, he was making arrangements to fly to Georgetown.

Expecting that a meeting with Board representatives would be useful, I requested one and Jeffrey Stollmeyer flew from Trinidad for it, along with Harold Burnett. Somehow, Peter Short, the Barbados delegate on the Board, was also in Georgetown at the time for a business meeting (another coincidence) and he sat in on a brief session which those WSC players who were in Georgetown at the time (Croft, Garner and Greenidge) and I had with the officials from the Board. Their position was as intransigent as ever, we heard nothing new and the meeting served no purpose whatever. The impasse was irrevocable.

When Kerry did arrive, along with Rudi Webster, he held a press conference at which he revealed that WSC was striving to work something out with the Indian Board over playing dates which would have allowed all those West Indians under contract to his group to be available for the West Indies team to India. It only needed a shift of about two weeks in the proposed itinerary to make the accommodation. Unfortunately, the Boards appeared unprepared to cooperate.

Even before the Test began, I had packed my bags and left for Manchester, passing in transit through Barbados where, that weekend, Kerry arranged for all WSC West Indian players to stay at the plush Sandy Lane Hotel and to bring along with them wives or girl friends, all at his expense. The

114

whole episode, he said, had been a pretty harrowing
psychological experience for professional cricketers who
had lost a lot by their decision, not only financially, but also
in terms of the satisfaction and pride of playing for their
country. Now they needed to relax and forget their
immediate worries.

His detractors said it was more Packer flash, another
attempt to dazzle everyone with his wealth. As far as the
players were concerned, however, it was a gesture much
appreciated, for we did relax and we did, to a large extent,
discard the worries of the recent past.

Certainly I felt a great relief at having taken my decision.
It was not a particularly easy one to make for I dearly wanted
to continue playing for the West Indies, in that series against
Australia even more so, and I was looking forward to
skippering them in a Test in Georgetown, having been
injured in the one the year before. But I knew that it would
have been impossible to have lived with my conscience if I
had gone along with the suspect policy of selection for that
third Test.

As was only to be expected, the issue created an immense
and immediate furore throughout the West Indies. A group
in Trinidad, calling itself the Committee for the Defence of
West Indies Cricket, wrote to me, giving strong support to
my position and informing me that it was mounting a
boycott of the fourth Test at the Queen's Park Oval. The
press and radio were filled with comments from everyone
from prime ministers to postmen and there were fears, mainly
from the overseas press I might add, that there would
be a violent reaction.

Physically, there was violence which stopped the final Test
in Jamaica but, from all reports, that was not triggered by
the issue over my resignation, but by an unfavourable
umpiring decision against the West Indies. I was long since
back in Manchester by then so I could only go by second-
hand reports on the incident. Verbally, too, there seemed to
be a lot of violence between those who were *for* the players
and those who were *against*. Again, I could only go from
what I read in the press and from what friends in the West
Indies reported back, which was just as well since I would not
like to have been embroiled in the arguments back and forth.

115

The majority of former players chose to say nothing, which I imagine was only natural. Nevertheless, several had privately told me and the other WSC players during our tour through the West Indies how glad they were that cricketers had finally made the breakthrough in realistic fees which players in tennis, golf, soccer and other sports had enjoyed for some time.

One man who did speak out forcibly in our favour, however, from the very beginning and all the way through was Wes Hall, an amiable and worldly character, with a magnetic personality, quick wit and keen intellect. Like all the players I know, I had always admired him and respected the opinions and advice always so freely given. The support of someone held in such high esteem was valued by myself and all the other players during that difficult period.

For months afterwards – and even sometimes now – I still look back to that fateful Easter weekend in Georgetown in 1978 and ask myself what my attitude would be had I to make the decision all over again in identical circumstances, with the benefit of hindsight. If anything, time has convinced me that I made the correct decision. It was one based on principle and the one which I will always believe to have been the proper one.

The fact that, within a year, I was reappointed West Indies captain may have been some vindication of the stand which I and my fellow WSC players took at the time, but whether or not I ever got back the captaincy or played Test cricket again is beside the point. My resignation was something which I knew, within myself, was right – and that was all that mattered.

12   Together Again

The cricket world continued in a state of turmoil throughout
1978 and into 1979. None of the established boards of
control appeared to grasp the significance of World Series
Cricket or to appreciate why virtually all the world's leading
players had agreed to play for it. To them, WSC was a threat
to their authority and should be quashed.

After we had withdrawn from the West Indies team, not a
single WSC player was involved in Test cricket. England, the
least affected of the major countries, humiliated a Pakistani
team without Majid, Asif, Mushtaq, Zaheer and Imran.
They also defeated New Zealand in England and did the
same in a devalued Ashes series in Australia during the
Australian summer of 1978/9, the margin being 5–1. The
West Indies, carrying several players who had hardly made
their names at Shield level, struggled through a tough series
in India, losing the only Test which produced a definite
result but hanging on for draws by the skin of their teeth in
two or three others.

It was a ludicrous situation, and we all wondered just how
long it could continue. As far as the West Indian public was
concerned, not very long at all. Members of the Barbados
Cricket Association and the Jamaica Cricket Association,
angered by what was happening to our cricket, summoned
meetings of their organizations and passed resolutions
which, in effect, called for the return of the best players to the
Test team and some agreement between the International
Cricket Conference and World Series Cricket.

The West Indies Board itself suffered financially because
of the impasse as crowds for the final three Tests of the series
against Australia fell dramatically, the boycott in Trinidad
being so effective that barely 1000 turned up at the Queen's
Park Oval for the fourth Test.

In the meantime, moves were being made for WSC to
bring a series to the West Indies during the 1979 season. A
group of Jamaican businessmen, headed by Pat Terralonge,
Franz Botek and Connie Pine, realized that Caribbean
cricket-lovers wanted to see a match between the two best
teams Australia and the West Indies could field; after initial

opposition from the West Indies Board and one or two local associations, the pressure of public opinion held sway. Even before we returned to Australia in November for WSC's second season there, we knew that we would be again playing before West Indian crowds in a series of five Supertests against Australia between mid February and mid April.

Yet the situation remained most unsavoury, and I think I speak for most of the players when I say that we were relieved when we heard of discussions between WSC and ICC representatives and when, towards the end of the WSC season in Australia, we received letters from the West Indies Board asking whether we would be available for the World Cup tournament in England scheduled for the following June.

As I saw it, we were recalled so hastily by the West Indies Board for two main reasons. The first was the outright condemnation which the Board had received everywhere from the cricketing public, reflected in the resolutions passed by the Barbados and Jamaica associations. The second was financial expediency. Without the leading players, the Board had lost heavily and its bank balances had deteriorated from something like £150,000 in the black to a healthy sum in the red. People were simply not going to pay to watch substandard cricket at Test level.

Our reply to the invitation to be available for the World Cup was a joint one. Following my resignation from the captaincy, the WSC players had acted collectively in withdrawing and it was only to be expected that we acted similarly in deciding on our return. There were still matters to be thrashed out, such as fees and the captaincy, which would be left for the Caribbean where we could meet directly with the Board. As far as the captaincy was concerned, the feeling was that since we were being reinstated, we should revert to the position prior to my resignation and that I should be reappointed. In principle, however, we all agreed that we would be available.

When I got to Port-of-Spain in March, during the WSC tour, I met with Jeffrey Stollmeyer, the first time we had spoken since our parting of the ways in Georgetown a year earlier. The first thing he said to me as he shook my hand

118

was: 'Let's let bygones be bygones. What has passed is all water under the bridge.' He was charming and I got the distinct impression that he realized that the Board's initial stand was a mistake. It is true that he attended none of the WSC matches on that tour but that was his prerogative. Yet he remained President of the West Indies Board and, as such, was committed to seeing our cricket flourish in every sense of the word. It was obvious it could only do that if all of its best players were available.

This realization was slowly sinking in with all ICC members particularly Australia, where crowds for the Ashes series against England were far lower than they had ever been while those at WSC matches were growing all the time. Somehow, people in England were being given the wrong impression about the impact of WSC, and the accuracy of the press reporting there left a lot to be desired. Yet officials in Australia with the England team, such as the manager, Doug Insole, could see for themselves and give a true account of how official Australian cricket was suffering in more ways than one.

Its second season must have astounded those who had written WSC off as a seven-day wonder even before it began. Anyone who was willing to be realistically objective would have conceded that it needed time to catch on. A century of tradition behind Test cricket is hard to break and there is no doubt that WSC struggled throughout its first year. In year two, however, inhibitions had broken down. In addition, mainly through promotion and television, WSC had attracted new followers to cricket, and that had to be a good thing.

The big breakthrough came when we played against the Australians in the first night match at the Sydney Cricket Ground. WSC had been granted use of the famous Test ground by the ground's trust amidst tremendous controversy and that in itself was a major acquisition. Lights were installed and there was great publicity for the game, particularly since the teams were fitted out in coloured clothing for the first time.

What an occasion it was. Thousands came along, attracted like moths to the lights. Many more may just have wanted to see what all the fuss was about. Hopefully, the vast majority came to see the cricket. By the time the lights went on, there were people everywhere and, soon, a gate had given way under the pressure and thousands flooded into the ground. There could be no accurate count but it was estimated that there were close to 50,000 that night and, unfortunately for us, they went home elated at an Australian victory.

We did not get that kind of crowd again during the season, yet on two occasions at VFL Park in Melbourne close to 40,000 turned out and the average attendance for all matches was over 10,000.

The cricket itself proved far tougher for us than it had been in the first year. We suffered a string of crucial injuries which affected our overall performances and emphasized the value of having the three additional players signed up during the Australian tour of the West Indies. The pitches, for some reason, were not up to first-class standard – with the exception, I might add, of John Maley's hot-house wonder at VFL Park which was always easier for batting than elsewhere. The two Test centres which we were now using, the SCG and the Gabba ground in Brisbane, favoured the bowlers far too much to ensure fair contests.

With more night matches and someone's misguided idea that the Supertests should run for seven hours, from 1.30 p.m. to 10.30 p.m. with an hour's break for dinner, the schedule was the toughest I have known – and trust will ever know. Perhaps that had a lot to do with the overall drop in performances, especially by the batsmen, and the injuries. Poor Joel Garner had to bowl something like thirty-six overs on the first day of the Supertest against the World team after Michael Holding tore a hamstring muscle early in the day, and he was never the same after that. Again, there was the problem of getting to sleep in the early hours of the morning after a night match – and having to be ready to leave the hotel by noon the next day.

There were those in WSC who also seemed to believe that the promotions were more important than the cricket. We would be summoned to make appearances for this company or that organization or to do a coaching stint at the most inopportune of times. We had an incredible situation in the first Supertest against the World team in Sydney when we decided, at the last minute, to play Albert Padmore, since the pitch indicated that a spinner would be needed. Paddy was nowhere to be found as he was out doing some promotion and we had to use a substitute until he could be rounded up!

We were knocked out in the Supertests by losing both to the World team and to the Australians in the preliminary matches. The World side had been boosted by the inclusion of Garth le Roux, a big South African fast bowler who proved the find of the season, Clive Rice, another South African who was an extremely useful all-rounder and the Pakistanis, Javed Miandad, Haroon Rashid and Sarfraz Nawaz. It was a very strong combination indeed and proved itself by beating both the West Indies and Australia in the Supertests. However, I do not rate it quite as powerful as the World team which had played in England during the 1970 season.

As far as we were concerned, we were let down by our batting. The only innings of any real note was Rowe's 175 in the Supertest against Australia in Melbourne, the type of knock which brought back memories of his early days when everything seemed to come so easily to him.

Consolation was in the International Cup, the limited-over competition. We only just managed to scrape through the Grand Finals which were to be the best of five matches, all at VFL Park. We lost the first, won the next two, and appeared certain to lose the fourth at 132 for six, replying to 240 off fifty overs. Somehow, I managed to find the type of form which had eluded me all season and, with help from Julien, Roberts and Garner on the field, and some acute mathematical calculations in the dressing rooms, we pulled off a stunning victory.

Perhaps the most stunned of all were the Australians. They had the game wrapped up but were given the wrong trail to victory when a message was sent on to the field from WSC's managing director, Andrew Caro, informing them that the match would continue until they bowled all their fifty overs. Since regulations stated play had to close at 10.25 p.m., there was no way they could have finished their quota without this intervention and the match would have to be decided on run-rate.

No one bothered to tell us of the proposed change and we

121

would not have fallen for it in any case. Rules are rules, and we were not going to have them amended. The first indication we had that something fishy was going on was when the lights on the scoreboard clock were switched off, apparently so we would be unaware of the time. However, we took it all along that run-rate would be the final decider and, when he came out to bat, Joel Garner produced a piece of paper on which was noted the target score we needed at the end of each over up to forty-eight.

By then, I was almost crippled by a pulled muscle in the thigh so that Austin was running for me and, between the three of us, we managed to get the required runs to see us home. At 10.25, as per regulations, the umpires called off the match and Austin and Garner – and, apparently, everyone in the dressing room as well – went delirious with delight while Ian Chappell and the Australians walked off as if they had been struck by lightning. Kerry Packer, I understand, had to do a lot of explaining to the Australians that night.

Little did we know it was to be the last major WSC match for all of us in Australia and that our days and nights at VFL Park were at an end.

Just one final comment about that last WSC season and it concerns the coloured clothing. A lot of the detractors said that they were all part of the razzle-dazzle and the circus act for television. In fact, there was a very practical reason for it. In the first season, the umpires and some of the players complained that the white ball would get 'lost' in the backdrop of white pads and white clothing. It was difficult for umpires to decide, for instance, on the height of the ball as it hit the pads or for a gully fielder to sight the ball early enough with the batsman's body behind it. The sightscreen had been darkened so the next step was to darken the clothing, making it coloured.

We all accepted the reason for it and, personally, I liked the effect. However, nobody in the West Indies camp was consulted as to what our colour would be and they bedecked us in something they called 'coral pink', but which would have been dubbed 'pansy pink' back in the West Indies where it has distinctly homosexual connotations. 'Packer's Pink Panthers' someone labelled us while there was a lot of ribbing in the dressing room when we put them on. I thought

'Big Bird' Garner looked decidedly cute! Nevertheless, we didn't mind wearing the new strip – as long as it was not in front of West Indian crowds!

Thankfully, there was no night cricket and no white ball for the WSC West Indies tour which followed immediately. It was very much back to the traditional game and, at most venues, there were even officials from the local Association and West Indies Board representatives assisting with the organization. Overall, however, there was a WSC committee of Pat Terrelonge, Franz Botek and Connie Pine, and their inexperience in putting on a major cricket match, handling crowds and that sort of thing did lead to some problems along the way.

The tour was badly marred by crowd disturbances and subjected the players to too much travel.

Twice the Supertest in Barbados was stopped by bottle-throwing spectators, the first time it had ever occurred at Kensington Oval; there was a bottle-throwing incident in the Trinidad Supertest as well; and then a full-scale riot in Guyana.

There was a combination of reasons for all three. In the first place, the people were extremely eager to see the teams in action. We were accepted as the best the West Indies and Australia could put out and the crowds, which seemed to view the matches as indeed Supertests, something even beyond Test cricket, were big everywhere. As a result of this, they apparently felt that we should have played even in conditions which were unsuitable for top-class cricket.

This was certainly the case in Georgetown and, to a lesser extent, in Bridgetown. In both instances, the outfield was wet following rain, and the umpires were quite right in waiting for conditions to improve before starting. In Bridgetown there was a lack of communication with a large Saturday afternoon crowd for which WSC officials must take full blame. Not knowing when play would restart, the crowd became restless and vented their feelings by throwing bottles.

In Georgetown, heavy rain for several days caused the start of the match to be postponed for two days. When the weather broke and the sun shone, WSC personnel, unaware of ground conditions, put it about that play would commence on schedule on the Sunday. When we got to the ground, the stands were already almost full but, as soon as I walked on to the ground, I knew play would only be possible very late in the day, if at all. It may have looked playable on the surface, which is all the public see, but it was very soft and dangerous underfoot. There were suggestions that we could have played and reduced our run-ups but this would have been out of the question in an important match.

Several people there were looking for the slightest problem to incite trouble. They were totally against WSC and were hoping to see it embarrassed, even if it meant sullying their country's good name in the process. Here was their opportunity and they got their satisfaction when the crowd exploded, breaking down fences, hurling bottles, benches and other debris on to the ground and storming the pavilion. It was not a happy experience, particularly as both teams were trapped in their dressing rooms for long periods. I had seen trouble at West Indian grounds before during my career but nothing like this and, especially since it was in Guyana, it left me very depressed.

Yet I am convinced that there were those who relished it and, the next day, they seized an opportunity to charge Ian Chappell with assault and the use of indecent language. The incident, as far as I was concerned, was blown out of all proportion, but this served the purpose of those intent on heaping scorn on WSC. All sorts of wild stories were spread, and when I tried to use my influence to defuse the situation I was told that the matter had already gone to 'higher authority'. Ian was taken to court and fined and, I imagine, a lot of people wrung their hands in glee.

Two other incidents, one in Barbados and the other in Trinidad, related to umpiring decisions against our batsmen which gave the impression that the crowds could not stand to see the West Indies lose. I do not think that was the case, particularly in Barbados. It was simply that there was a spate of umpiring mistakes which caused a lot of tension on the field, and this was transferred to the crowds. The ready availability of bottles at West Indian grounds provide perfect ammunition, and the relevant authorities will have to examine the possibility of selling drinks in paper cups in future. More than that, however, they should start providing spectators who watch the game for six hours a day with better amenities, certainly in the West Indies. Crowd behaviour the world over may have deteriorated, but people who have paid good money to watch cricket are not going to stop play for no reason. Perhaps the events during the WSC tour provided a lesson for everyone connected with cricket.

It was a pity that the cricket itself had to be over-shadowed because the series was very keenly fought and there was some very good cricket played. We won the first Supertest in Jamaica by the wide margin of 369 runs and, at long last, I found form at precisely the right moment. Fast bowling dominated the two first innings and we needed a big second innings total to be safe and, with the much improved Andy Roberts helping in a sixth-wicket stand of 226, I scored 197.

The crowd saw to it that the Barbados match was drawn; the Australians levelled the series by winning a close encounter in Trinidad; rain and the riot made the Guyana Supertest no more than an exhibition; and we just could not get through the second innings on a perfect batting pitch in Antigua in the fifth and final. In between all these, we were hop-scotching about the Caribbean for a succession of one-day matches which left everyone thoroughly fed up and exhausted by the end of it all. In addition to the Supertests, we played one-day games in all the main centres plus St Lucia, Berbice, Dominica and St Kitts.

Anyone with the faintest knowledge of communications between the West Indian islands will understand what an exacting schedule that was; it meant catching irregular flights at irregular hours, changing planes, going through the lengthy process of filling in immigration forms and driving long distances from airport to hotel. For a one-day match, it just didn't seem worth it.

Soon after the WSC tour had ended, the West Indies Board held its annual general meeting. At this it was decided that I should be reinstated as West Indies captain. The vote was by no means unanimous, and I am aware that there were those on the board who argued against my reappointment.

Even when the decision was finally made, the Board stipulated that I would have to play one match for Guyana in the Shell Shield, which I thought was very petty. It was not as if I was a new player just making my name and, in any case, the ruling did not apply to everyone since Kallicharran remained in England after the Indian tour.

Yet I was happy and, in many ways, relieved to have the job back since I was not certain how the WSC players, who were also named to form the nucleus of the squad for the second World Cup tournament in England in June, would have reacted had I been overlooked.

I was a little apprehensive initially about how the team spirit would be. After all, we had only just been in dispute with the Board; and Kallicharran, appointed captain for India when we were unavailable, had reverted to his former position as an ordinary team member – although subsequently named on the tour committee in England. While in India, the team under Kallicharran had informed the Board that it was opposed to its decision to consider WSC players for World Cup selection, an action which those of us with WSC found childish and aggravating.

In addition, Clyde Walcott, a member of the selection panel which made the omissions that triggered the impasse in the first place, was appointed team manager.

My concern was unfounded. I have always got along well with Clyde and found him to have a concern for the players, a knowledge of cricket and a personable manner. He had managed our team in the first World Cup and again on the England tour in 1976, and had proved extremely capable in that position, well liked and respected by the players. So it proved again on this occasion. The episode which led to the split between myself and the Board was no longer relevant and both sides treated it as such.

If there was any coolness towards Kalli and the other non-WSC players in the team – Faoud Bacchus, Larry Gomes and Malcolm Marshall – I certainly did not detect it. Kalli was an integral part of the team, as he always had been, and I was most impressed with Bacchus, Gomes and Marshall even though they did not play a single game. Far from moping and complaining, they were cheerful members of a cheerful team, taking part keenly in team discussions and being very helpful in other respects.

Having taken the first World Cup in 1975, I felt even more confident this time. Seven of those who played in that inaugural tournament survived – Deryck Murray, Green-

idge, Kallicharran, Richards, King, Roberts and myself –
and we had added to that list three other outstanding fast
bowlers – Holding, Croft and Garner. If we lacked the
number of all-rounders we had then, with Julien and Boyce
missing, we were certainly stronger in bowling.

In addition, most of us had played limited-over cricket as
a team consistently during the two seasons of World Series
Cricket and had won the WSC International Cup on both
occasions.

The draw was somewhat easier than in 1975 with India,
New Zealand and Sri Lanka in our group, leaving England,
Pakistan, a depleted Australia, and a Canadian team
comprised mostly of West Indian immigrants to battle it out
in the other.

Our only stumbling block in the first round was the
weather, which completely washed out our scheduled match
against Sri Lanka at the Oval. At Edgbaston we easily
defeated India, and at Trent Bridge we won against a plucky
and very efficient New Zealand team.

As far as most people were concerned the best match in the
competition was our semi-final against Pakistan. It was a
magnificent day at the Oval and the batsmen on both teams
did not disappoint a big crowd. However, once we had
amassed 291 for eight from our sixty overs after Asif Iqbal
had sent us in, I had no fears about losing. I realized that
players like Majid, Zaheer, Asif, Javed Miandad, Haroon
and Imran could score quickly, but I defy any team in the
world to score at almost 5 runs an over, over sixty overs,
against our attack.

There was a time, just before a very late tea break, when
Majid and Zaheer were going along so smoothly that the
West Indian cheering section, usually so noisy, had become
strangely silent. The interval was just what we needed for we
pulled ourselves together, decided on a leg-stump attack and
quickly got the wickets we needed. Once Zaheer was caught
down the leg-side off Croft and Majid caught at cover, there
was never any doubt about the result.

So we were through to the Final again and this time
England would be the opposition. So versed in the one-day
stuff, England can never be underestimated, but I was
surprised at some of their tactics in a match which we won by

127

a large margin of 92 runs.

The fact that Mike Brearley sent us in on winning the toss was not as strange as was made out. Captains believe that a pitch prepared for a one-day match can only improve, and the trend has been to bowl first. When we were 99 for four just before lunch and making pretty heavy weather of it, no one questioned the wisdom of Brearley's move.

After lunch, however, Brearley had the problem of whether to go for the breakthrough with his leading bowlers with Richards and King as the only remaining specialist batsmen, thus risking his 'fill-in' bowlers in the closing stages of the innings, or whether to keep them in reserve. It is always a difficult decision and he opted to use Boycott, Gooch and Larkins, the bit bowlers, to his regret.

To tell the truth, I do not think any bowler would have bothered King in the mood he was in that day. He cracked the ball like thunder to all parts of the ground while Richards, at the other end, carried out the supporting role admirably. King plays his cricket as he lives his life. He is a human dynamo, full of energy and non-stop action. His batting may be unorthodox but he has a remarkable eye and incredible strength. By the time he was out for 85, one of the best innings I have seen in a match of this importance, we were 238 for five and I knew the match was ours.

Richards ended the innings in most dramatic fashion, with an improvised pull shot for six off Hendrick. He was 138 not out at the finish, a great performance by a great player who had promised us a big innings even before it began.

To win, England needed to score at a steady rate throughout their innings, but Boycott and Brearley placed far too much emphasis on a solid start. They got that all right, adding 129 for the first wicket, but they took too many overs to do so and put enormous pressure on the stroke-players who were to follow. I could have watched them all day as I knew every over they batted was another nail in their coffin. When I dropped Boycott from a rather comfortable catch at mid-on at one stage, there were a lot of people who suggested I put it down purposely just to keep him in. Not true – but it would not have been a bad tactic!

It was an excellent match, if not quite as exciting throughout as the Final in 1975. Again, there were thousands of West Indians at Lord's to boost us and to celebrate the victory afterwards.

It was a victory which meant even more than usual for West Indian cricket – and for me personally. We had all gone through a difficult period and this was the perfect way to signal an end to the problems. West Indies cricket was now back on its feet again.

Yet again, however, our victory was treated in a very matter-of-fact way by the Board. It was almost as if everyone in the West Indies took it as a foregone conclusion that we would win and we all simply went our different ways when it was all over. At least in 1975, the Prudential Trophy was displayed throughout the West Indies and the event was marked by the issuing of a stamp. Now there was nothing – except the satisfaction of a job well done and the tournament fee.

Perhaps, after all, the Board had learned nothing from the WSC impasse about improving its relationships with the players. I personally was staggered when Clyde Walcott came up to me before the tournament started and said he had been authorized by the Board to offer me £50 as captain's fee. At first, I thought he was joking and I knew he felt a little embarrassed by it. If that was what they felt the captaincy was worth, it was better that they made no offer at all, I told Clyde.

In the end, he came back to offer £100, which was hardly a princely sum either, but that was not the point. There was a principle involved. In the end, I accepted the final offer, although yet again I could not help but shake my head in disbelief at the thinking behind a Board decision.

13   Australian Revenge

Ever since our defeat at the hands of Australia in 1975–6, I had longed for the opportunity to prove to everyone, not least myself, that it was one of those inexplicable happenings in sport.

World Series Cricket had brought virtually the same teams together again for two seasons in Australia and for one in the West Indies, and the results in the Supertests had been absolutely even – two victories each and a draw in Australia; one victory each with the other matches drawn in the five Supertests in the Caribbean.

Yet, for the cricketing world and for myself as well, it was not the same thing, since neither Australia nor ourselves were selecting from *all* the best players. Now, with the settlement between WSC and the International Cricket Conference, Test cricket would be Test cricket again and, during the World Cup, the new feeling of anticipation among most of the world's players could be felt.

The Australian Board, which had suffered very badly financially in the two seasons during which it competed with WSC, was naturally anxious to recoup some of its losses. The contract which it struck with the Channel Nine television network ensured a sizeable sum annually but it needed something out of the ordinary to put Test cricket back on its feet again, while at the same time taking advantage of the new popularity of limited-over cricket, particularly under lights.

So England and the West Indies were both invited for a three-way series to join Australia in what was to be called the World Series Cup limited-over competition and each to play a three-Test series against the home team.

I was particularly confident this time that all the frustrations suffered by West Indian teams in Australia in the past could be put behind us. It was a fact that all five previous West Indies touring teams dating back to 1930–1 had returned from Australia defeated, for a variety of reasons, but this time I knew it would change.

We had a strong, united team, with plenty of experience of the conditions we could expect. Eleven of us had played in

Australia during the previous two seasons with World Series; several had been in the 1975–6 side, and wanted to avenge that loss as much as I did. In addition to those who had been with WSC, there was Kallicharran, who would boost our batting and who also had plenty of Australian experience, Larry Gomes, who had done very well in the West Indies team when it played without the WSC men, David Murray, the reserve keeper, Derek Parry, the specialist spinner and a worthy all-rounder, and Malcolm Marshall who was retained as the fifth fast bowler from the World Cup.

So I arrived in Australia in early November full of hope. By the end of the month, I was wondering whether I would ever play any serious cricket again, far less take part in a series to which I had been so looking forward.

The problem was that old, creaking right knee of mine. I had had the cartilage removed in England during the summer of 1977 but it had never recovered its full strength and was inclined to become swollen and painful after a long session in the field or a long innings.

It was not that I had many long innings early on the tour, yet the problem – and the pain – became more acute with every match. I desperately wanted to continue playing but it soon became obvious that this simply wouldn't be possible. After our first two limited-over matches, I had to have the knee strapped as I lay on a table in the dressing room for half-hour or more before I could even move.

Finally, I could no longer delay what doctors termed 'an exploratory operation'. They told me they would use a new technique known as micro-surgery. Only a very tiny cut would be necessary and, if successful, I could be playing again within a fortnight. It seemed as if I had heard that type of medical opinion before, and I took this one with a pinch of salt as well.

It was on the eve of the first Test and I was completely down in the dumps when the team left Sydney for Brisbane to prepare for the match, leaving me behind for an operation which could decide my future. To my delight and, I must admit, surprise, the doctors lived up to their word. The cut from the operation needed only a couple of stitches, the offending matter was removed from the knee with what I understood to be the medical equivalent of a vacuum cleaner, the contents presented to me in a bottle and, within two days, I was surprising everyone by turning up at the Gabba ground in Brisbane to watch the progress of the first Test.

As luck would have it, I was greeted by a power strike which put all the lifts at our hotel out of action, but when I managed to get down fourteen flights of stairs to the ground from my room with the aid of crutches, and without much bother, I knew I was on the mend.

As the doctors promised, I was back on the field within two weeks, playing against Tasmania at Launceston – and scoring 77 to boot – and a few days later actually bowling in a World Series Cup match, something I hadn't done in a serious match for a few years.

My luck had changed and, it seemed, just about that time the team's luck also changed.

We had not started very well, losing our first two limited-over matches, not managing to convert an excellent position in the first Test into victory, receiving a bad and, most of the time, unfair press and left to wonder, yet again, about the quality of the umpiring.

The opening of the World Series Cup put us against Australia at Sydney; even though we did not bat well in scoring 193, Australia were struggling at 52 for four when we were positive Greg Chappell was caught behind off his first ball from Michael Holding. It was the prize wicket and our memories quickly flashed back to a similar incident involving Greg's brother, Ian, at the same ground in the Test four seasons earlier. As it was, Greg was given not out and led them home with an unbeaten 74.

We were naturally upset, but we were staggered when the press next day claimed we had kicked down the dressing-room door and when I was criticized for not attending the presentation ceremony afterwards. The truth was that the door was not very strong and had come off the hinges several times during the season. It did so again as someone tried to force it when it was locked. As far as I was concerned, I could hardly walk with my crocked knee. But the journalists did not worry to check out these falsehoods with us.

In the second match, we went down to England on the last

ball. We needed 3 off it to win; England's captain Mike Brearley set everyone on the boundary including the wicketkeeper, Bairstow, and Ian Botham finished off the match by bowling Colin Croft.

Brearley's defensive action infuriated Australians who, by this time, had come to despise the Englishmen even more than ever. I had heard, over the years, of the antagonism between the Aussies and the 'Poms' during an Ashes series and I expected it would be in evidence again. But I do feel Brearley brought much of it on his team this time by refusing to accept the majority of the innovations suggested to them by the Australian Board.

England vetoed the idea of the thirty-metre circles used in World Series Cricket which had been so popular. They opted not to wear the new striped, coloured gear. They prevented the use of the white ball in all limited-over matches. Too much experimenting, they said, and yet they had refused to play for the Ashes precisely because they termed it an experimental series. It seemed to me as if they wanted to have their cake and eat it too.

In the first Test, we secured a big first innings lead but then centuries by Greg Chappell and Hughes kept us at bay. Our batting revolved around Richards's magnificent 140, a sign of things to come, for he played as he had done in England in 1976 for the rest of the series.

We were handicapped by an easy-paced pitch, a vital dropped catch off Greg Chappell when he was at 21 of his second innings 124 and, just possibly, by the lack of a spinner. Selection was difficult, for the Brisbane pitch tends to become slower and slower throughout and we were unsure whether to go for all pace as usual. I don't know what I would have done in the end for I would have needed to hear the rest of the selection committee put their views. However, I was never consulted by them as I was in Sydney when they deliberated, a discourtesy which upset me at the time. After all, I could have been contacted by telephone quite easily. As it was, I was not playing: Deryck Murray took over the captaincy and, having not been consulted either, I really felt on the outside.

By the time the second Test came around, we had rather mixed fortunes in the World Series Cup matches, beating

Australia very comfortably at Melbourne when Richards compiled a thrilling 153 not out in quite masterful style and beating England equally easily at Brisbane where Greenidge joined Richards in a feast of strokeplay. Yet we allowed an excellent position against Australia at Sydney in a night match to slip away; we lost by 7 runs as I marked my return to international competition with a duck.

With this inconsistency, there was some real doubt as to whether we would even qualify for the finals of the World Series Cup. The two top teams at the end of the first round of the matches would advance and, in the end, to make it we needed some help from England, who beat Australia every time in that first round. Yet I felt sure once we were through we would win the Cup and the prize money.

For all of us, however, the Tests were still the major consideration. Although the limited-over game has gained importance over the years, there is still nothing to match the status of Test cricket and, after Australia's escape in the first Test, we were even more intent than ever on winning at Melbourne to take a crucial lead.

The West Indies had never before won a Test at Melbourne but this time we broke the jinx. Although we thought we would require a spinner, the four fast bowlers were able to remove the Australians cheaply in both innings. With Richards again leading the way and with everybody down the line chipping in, we established a winning first innings lead.

At our team meetings and in private conversation, we had worked out our plan of attack carefully.

I had a system of switching around the fast bowlers so that two would always be fresh. In addition, I was always careful not to bowl any one of them into the ground although, with the low Australian totals, there was never much danger of this. At the end of the series, no more than fifteen overs separated the four of them.

We proved a few things to ourselves in that second Test, and the most significant was Greg Chappell's vulnerability to the bouncer. The pitch was uneven in bounce and Garner, who troubled him most, is a difficult customer much of the time. But we already had our suspicions about Chappell's ability to handle the rising, chest-high ball, which we used with good effect. In the third Test, Roberts served him one first ball and, squaring up, he got it on the splice for a catch to gully.

Before that third Test, we had the finals of the World Series Cup to think of. England were our opponents and, man for man, we knew we should have little trouble. However, the Englishmen keenly appreciate the tactics required for this type of cricket and we were by no means complacent.

In the first match, in fact, we barely scraped through. By now, Gordon Greenidge was in really magnificent form, his bat seeming a yard wide, and his 80 was mainly responsible for our 215 for eight off our fifty overs.

We had been having problems with our fifth bowler, for Collis King seemed to have lost his confidence and Richards was inconsistent. I had to break up ten overs between them and these were inevitably proving expensive. They conceded 74 runs to be exact, but Roberts, Garner and Croft managed to check the scoring at the end so that some real slogging was needed if England were to get the runs.

With 14 required off the last over from Holding, I had no real worries. However, Brearley and Bairstow played so well that they reduced it to a boundary off the last ball. Amidst tremendous tension, Holding was on line and Brearley could only get it into the outfield for two, Bairstow being run out on an impossible third. So we scraped home.

There was no way we were going to let this happen again in the second match at Sydney two days later. Greenidge and Richards, our two outstanding batsmen for the season, saw us home by eight wickets, a triumph worth Aus.$32,000 to the team kitty.

Unfortunately, I hadn't contributed much myself and, when we arrived in Adelaide, the doubts which haunt all batsmen short of runs were surfacing. When a journalist asked me how long I thought I had in Test cricket just before the start of the game, I smiled and replied: 'Oh, about five days, I suppose.' It was a flippant remark but it showed the way I was feeling.

My attitude was to change in a few hours with the satisfaction of a long-overdue Test match century. It is remarkable how any sportsman can be affected emotionally by success and failure, but when I walked to the middle at the Adelaide Oval for that innings, with the West Indies quite suddenly struggling at 126 for four, my form was poor and I was really worried.

Perhaps this was just as well for it made me more determined and more careful in my approach. We could not lose this match and, as Lawrence Rowe and myself set about restoring the innings, we both appreciated the situation. Neither of us had any sort of form and we both scratched around for a long time, knowing that if we got out cheaply Australia would take control of the match.

As so often happens, my form and confidence came back during the course of the innings and I went on to get 121, a knock which gave me as much pleasure as any I can remember. It was crucial to the course of the match and set us on our way to a really crushing victory by 408 runs.

The fast bowlers again did their jobs magnificently, and Australia tumbled for 203. As we built up our lead, with more runs from Greenidge and Richards and Kallicharran's first century of the series, there were questions as to when I would declare. We went 400 ahead, 450 ahead, 470 ahead, 500 ahead.

However, all West Indians knew what it was to suffer at the hands of Australia in Test cricket and I remember Bill Lawry setting us over 700 to win in Sydney in 1968-9. There was plenty of time remaining as we kept on going past lunch on the fourth day and, in the end, no declaration was necessary. Little did those who were suggesting it know that Vivian Richards was in the dressing room advising me to 'give them 1000 to win, skipper'. And I don't think he was wholly joking!

With a daunting 573 to make, with a day and a half remaining, the Australians did not have much spirit in their second innings while we were anxious to get it over quickly. I knew what it must have felt like for I had been on the receiving end before. Now it was gratifying to be on top and when the fast bowlers routed them for 165 in their second innings we had completed the heaviest victory ever recorded by West Indies over Australia – and, more importantly, had become the first West Indies team to clinch a series down-under.

The feeling of sporting revenge is sweet indeed and, as the champagne corks popped in our dressing room and the mood became merrier and merrier and the noise louder and louder, it was nice simply to sit back and savour it.

It was nice, too, to hear people like Richie Benaud compare us with the greatest of all West Indies teams and also refer to us along with Bradman's magnificent Australian side of 1948.

We had played almost to our peak throughout the three Tests, and everyone contributed. Perhaps Richards's brilliance tended to overshadow the other batsmen but all of them played important innings more than once. Our fast bowlers, in their differing ways, kept the pressure on the batsmen all the time, and our fielding and catching could scarcely be faulted. In addition, we did not have to chop and change the team as we had been forced to do in 1975–6 because of injury, using only thirteen players in the three Tests this time.

It is probably true that the Australians were below their strength of four seasons earlier and undoubtedly suffered from the injuries to Thomson and Hogg which denied Lillee support. Yet Lillee remains a magnificent bowler and Greg Chappell a world-class batsman. Laird, that most resolute of opening batsmen, and Hughes, more dashing in his approach, were both good enough to have been in the 1975–6 side. And it should not be forgotten that Australia trounced England 3–0 in the series which ran concurrently with ours.

Whether the three-way idea was such a good thing, I am not altogether sure. The interspersing of so many limited-over matches between the Tests upset a number of players who found it difficult to adjust their game accordingly, while I was told more than once that the public was unsure which type of match was being played where and involving whom. In the future, it would probably be better to plan the limited-over tournament over a set period before the Test series start or after they finish and also to separate the two series as is done in England during a shared tour.

That is my advice to the Australian Board. My advice to the West Indies Board is never again to schedule a New Zealand tour immediately after an Australian one.

At any time, an Australian series is tough. At the end of it touring teams simply want to get back home, whether they have done well or badly. For the second time I was in a team which faced a short, three-Test stint in New Zealand tacked on after an Australian tour, and on neither occasion did we have the heart for it.

In 1968-9, we had been beaten in Australia and were pretty much down in the dumps when we reached New Zealand, where we found it difficult to lift our game. On this occasion, we left Australia on a high and, even before it started, there was the general feeling that New Zealand would be anti-climax.

As it turned out, it was much more than just an anti-climax. It was a pure disaster.

In the thirty-four days we spent there, we played on twenty-four days in six different cities and had three Tests included. On pitches and in a climate entirely different from Australia's, the period for adjustment was extremely short. Yet we are all professional cricketers with plenty of experience and, like other teams in the past who have crossed the Tasman Sea to undertake a similar venture, we would have to grin and bear it and try to do our best.

Soon we discovered that our best was not going to be good enough in view of a never-ending succession of staggering umpiring decisions which went against us, match after match. It did not matter how hard we tried, we were thwarted every time by crucial decisions.

We were alarmed at first by the low standard of umpiring which we encountered and became more and more frustrated as it seemed clear we were getting the raw end of the deal. Gradually, that frustration turned to understandable anger and, finally, to a resignation that we would have to abide by it, regardless of how bad it was.

Midway during the third day of the second Test at Christchurch, however, we found that we could take it no more.

We had been beaten in the first test at Dunedin by one wicket and a magnificent job by our bowlers had come to nothing, almost certainly on account of the umpiring. In a low-scoring match, New Zealand needed only 104 to win but Holding, Croft and Garner, in the absence of the injured

Roberts, responded magnificently to the challenge and when New Zealand were 54 for seven victory appeared ours against all the odds. Then Cairns, a dangerous hitter at No. 9, got what seemed a big nick to Garner before he had scored and Murray took the catch; astonishingly umpire Fred Goodall turned down our appeal.

As it turned out, Cairns went on to make 19 crucial runs. Earlier, a seemingly clear-cut catch by Deryck Murray off Holding against John Parker had been refused by umpire John Hastie. Holding, an intense competitor, was so incensed he kicked over the stumps to release his pent-up emotions.

I would be the first to admit that we did not bat well and that New Zealand's fine fast bowler, Richard Hadlee, bowled superbly in the conditions. Yet it is pertinent that six of his eleven victims in that match were leg before.

Again we struggled for runs in the second Test and were all out for 228 but again our fast bowlers struck back on a pitch which maintained a little life into the third day. New Zealand were 53 for three but their captain, Geoff Howarth, and John Parker, two experienced players, began to pull them round as we shouted ourselves hoarse in unsuccessful appeal after unsuccessful appeal. The most controversial decision came when Howarth edged Garner to Murray when he was 68, and was given not out.

He had reached 99 by tea and was well entrenched. By this time, there was a feeling of absolute bitterness among us all. In addition to everything else, umpire Goodall was calling no-ball when it was clear it wasn't one and we felt – and I am sure this was not an emotional opinion formed in the heat of the moment – that we were being got at.

By the time we reached the dressing room, we were at the end of our tether. We were convinced, by now, that, no matter what, we could not win.

So what could we do about it? Some suggested that we seek to have umpire Goodall replaced. Some said it was best that the match and the tour be called off. Some were prepared not to go back on to the field. Finally, we decided to go back out, assuring everyone that we would discuss the matter on the rest day, and we took the field ten minutes after schedule. It was reported as a protest but there had been certainly no deliberate action to delay our return to the middle.

When we did resume, it was impossible to motivate the players. They just went through the motions, ambling around with no sense of purpose. Their spirits, all of our spirits, had been broken.

At close of play, there was still a strong body of opinion that the tour should be abandoned and most of the gear was even moved from the dressing room that evening in case such a decision should be taken. Next day, we met for over three hours at our hotel with views coming from everyone. Willie Rodriguez, our manager, was in touch with two West Indies Cricket Board officials, Peter Short and the President, Jeffrey Stollmeyer, and the matter was thrashed out.

It was fortunate, I think, that it was a rest day and we could all look at things a little more dispassionately. In the end, all the repercussions of abandoning the tour were discussed and it was clear that the best thing would be to continue.

Unfortunately, there was no improvement in the umpiring and, on the following day, there was the much-publicized incident involving Croft and umpire Goodall, in which Croft, on his approach, bounced into the umpire. We apologized to the New Zealand Board and the umpire – for this unhappy incident and for Holding's action in kicking over the stumps in Dunedin.

By the time we came to the final Test, we had resigned ourselves to the inevitable spate of negative umpiring decisions, so much so that Holding asked: 'What's the use of appealing any more? You'll only get yourself laryngitis.' In that match, the left-handed opener Bruce Edgar scored 127 and six times he was lucky with umpiring decisions, all involving catches to Murray, including one off Croft after he had been stuck on 99 for half-an-hour.

By our reckoning, there were twelve decisions in the three Tests which went wrongly against us. Deryck Murray had no fewer than eight clear catches refused.

All of this is far from a reaction to our defeat. I have played cricket long enough all over the world to accept the good decisions and the bad, and to know there are times when the home team gets more than its fair share of the benefit. Our team in New Zealand did not comprise young

140

players with temperamental natures unaccustomed to the problems of overseas tours and overseas umpiring. We had all been through it before.

No, seasoned professional cricketers with careers and reputations to think of do not suggest abandoning a tour without just cause and without provocation. For those who accuse us of poor sportsmanship in New Zealand I would ask that they judge us by our previous record and suggest that there is only so much that any one man can take, no matter how strong his character.

To tell the truth, I feel a little sorry for New Zealand. Their cricket has undoubtedly improved in recent years and they are desperate to demonstrate to the world that they are no longer the cinderellas of Test cricket. However, they will never be accepted as such until their pitch conditions and the standard of their umpiring improves and until they can prove themselves overseas.

It is no coincidence that only two of New Zealand's Test victories have been achieved overseas. They have some outstanding players and the basis of a strong side, but they are being given a false sense of their ability by the favourable circumstances which obtain at home.

Unless they can put these things right, no one will accept the results they achieve at home and visiting teams will be reluctant to visit. And that will be a pity.

14   England and Pakistan

There was hardly time to get over the fatigue, and the controversy, of the tour to Australia and New Zealand before we faced almost a year of virtually uninterrupted Test cricket. There was a full tour of England in the summer of 1980, followed by a series of four Tests in Pakistan between early November and early January, always an exacting business, and then straight back home to face England again for five Tests during the West Indies season of 1981.

It might have appeared a pretty hectic schedule, particularly for someone in cricketing middle-age, but I was really looking forward to it. A tour of England, for obvious reasons, holds a special place in the hearts of West Indian cricketers, more especially these days when so many of us are resident there, at least for part of the year. The large West Indian community turns out in large numbers to give us their support and I can safely say that I have enjoyed every minute of my tours to England with West Indies' teams.

What is more, we had done particularly well under my captaincy, with the World Cup successes in 1975 and 1979 and the equally satisfying 3–0 victory over Tony Greig's team in 1976. Now we were returning to defend the Frank Worrell Trophy we had won then and, without in any way being complacent or arrogant, I felt we had a good enough team to justify the bookmakers' judgment in installing us as short-odds favourites.

That was to be followed by the first separate tour of Pakistan by the West Indies. We had always tacked on Pakistan at the end of an Indian tour, very much as we had done with New Zealand after Australia, and I felt that this was something of a slight to a country which had produced so many outstanding cricketers. Conditions for touring might not be the best but, as professional cricketers and as a team supposedly world champions, we have to be prepared to play everywhere and, knowing the Pakistanis' strength, I envisaged a hard-fought series with plenty of exciting batting on both sides.

Then it would be home for the first series against England since 1974. Why there should be such a lengthy break between visits by England to the Caribbean I am not certain but this was to be the first time that I would be skipper at home against the old enemy and there was bound to be enormous public interest.

So, there was a lot to look forward to. Unfortunately, expectations fell well short of reality and the cricket in all three series was spoiled and overshadowed by several factors, many of them of a highly emotional and controversial nature. Instead of it being a period of excitement and fulfilment for West Indies cricket and cricketers it turned out to be most disappointing.

The first furore, in fact, broke even before the tour of England began and, not for the first time and, certainly not for the last, concerned the selection of the team.

When the Trinidadian left-handed batsman Larry Gomes was omitted from the squad of sixteen, there was an immediate outcry in his native island. I could only go on press reports but, apparently, there were suggestions from high quarters there that Trinidad and Tobago withdraw from the Shell Shield in protest and the Cricket Council even recommended that players in its competitions should wear black arm bands. I know Trinidadians are an emotional people who tend to overreact when they feel they have been hard done by – but this was really carrying it too far.

So why did we decide to omit Gomes? To hear the Trinidadians tell it, it was because we had it in for them and, in fact, Gomes was a very talented player with real potential. However, he didn't appear interested on the tour of Australia and New Zealand when he seemed to be upset that he was in the reserves without a chance to make the Test or one-day teams. The fact was that the way the tour was scheduled there was little scope to bring in the reserve players, and he, David Murray and Malcolm Marshall had to sit it out for long periods.

In addition, at this stage, we were anxious to try new players in the middle order and we decided to carry Faoud Bacchus, a good cricketer who had scored 250 in his last Test innings in India when the bulk of the West Indies team was in Australia with World Series.

As it turned out, I think it gave Larry a very good kick up the pants and made him understand that he had to go in and

143

fight for his place. No player can be assured of a place in any Test eleven unless he keeps performing and unless he shows that he is keen. At that stage, we didn't feel Larry was keen enough. It is only necessary to look at his figures recently to see how much tougher he has become in his approach.

The repercussions were unfortunate but not surprising in the West Indies. However, as captain and a selector I cannot afford to think of what the public's reactions might be. You're in danger of developing clouded judgment if you start trying to please public opinion and, in any case, it is impossible to please all of the people all of the time – particularly West Indian people.

The England tour itself was almost completely submerged in one of the wettest and most miserable summers I had known in more than a decade playing there – and it should be noted that it didn't rain only in Manchester! Every Test was affected and the only one in which we had enough time for a result was the first at Trent Bridge in which we just managed to scrape home by two wickets.

What a contrast it was to the two previous tours, in 1973 and 1976, when the sun shone with Caribbean fury and brilliance and we matched it with our performances. Now we could get nothing going and we spent as much time huddled up in dressing rooms up and down the country waiting for the rain to stop and the umpires to inspect as we did on the field of play.

The first Test victory was a little too close for comfort and I was happy the ice-cool Andy Roberts was there at the end to steer us home. Played in overcast conditions and on an unusually green pitch, the ball behaved strangely and batting was never easy. My part in the match was restricted after I split the webbing between the first and second fingers on my right hand, unsighted when Deryck Murray came across me at first slip trying to make a catch. So I watched most of it from the pavilion.

In fact, injuries were another factor which made life miserable for me personally. In the first one-day international, I had come down hard on my behind and that did my back enough harm to keep me out for a week. Then, in the fourth Test at the Oval, I tore a hamstring chasing a ball in the outfield in England's first innings and that was it for the old warhorse for the rest of the tour, Richards taking over the captaincy for the rest of that match and for the final Test as well.

I did wonder at the time whether someone up there was trying to convey a message but I've been injured so many times in the past that I was long since past despairing. So I had a little chuckle when, watching the day's highlights on television after the first day of the Oval Test. I heard Richie Benaud speculate whether this would, finally, be the end for me.

There were those who suggested we were lucky to win that first test because England dropped a catch at a crucial stage – Roberts, when 13 were needed. Yet we put down crucial catches, too, and we gave them no fewer than 77 extras, still only needing 209 to win in the end.

In fact, our catching throughout was well below the high standards we had set earlier. The weather must take some of the blame for it is not easy to sight the ball on a dull, grey day when it comes flying off the edge from one of our fast bowlers. Yet you don't expect top-class catchers to miss as many as we did that series.

In the third Test at Manchester, Peter Willey was dropped at a crucial stage in England's second innings and in the fourth at the Oval Bob Willis was put down relatively early in a match-saving last wicket stand with Willey. On both occasions, the fielder was Gordon Greenidge in the slips and, normally, there is no better catcher there.

I did wonder at the time whether Gordon's concentration and attitude might not have been affected by the hornet's nest which the publication of his autobiography stirred up. It came on to the market the day the Old Trafford Test began and the first I knew about it was when the *Sun* newspaper carried extracts, with appropriately sensational headlines.

And sensational stuff it was! Sensational and personally hurtful to me and some of the other players.

Gordon had played all his Test cricket under me, since making his debut in 1974, and yet here, for the first time, I was to read that he felt all along that he could not confide in me nor ask for my advice.

'He had done nothing to help or reassure me in Australia, reserving his comments about me for the newspapers or for team meetings when he dished out nothing but criticism,' he wrote about one C.H. Lloyd. And there were other uncomplimentary statements, not only about me but about one or two other members of the team as well.

It took us all by surprise. I knew Gordon was a rather quiet, reserved individual who took failure hard and who was particularly upset by his experiences in Australia in 1975-6 when he had a bad tour. But I never expected this type of outburst – there in black and white, in his life story, on the eve of a Test match to boot.

Naturally, it had an effect on the atmosphere in the dressing room and things were pretty strained for a few days. It made me start to question myself. Was there something in what he said? Was I really unapproachable? Then I realized that the problem was not mine so much as Gordon's, a complex personality as revealed in his book. I had a job to do and would continue to do it to the best of my ability.

Gordon, in fact, was very upset with what had been published but surely he must have read through the proofs, even if he wanted to contend that his associate writer had misinterpreted what he had said. He was even willing to take it off the market but that would have been too costly an exercise and, in any case, the newspapers saw to it that the juicy parts were widely quoted.

It was probably significant that he dropped those crucial catches after that and that he went for a duck and 6 in his next two Test innings. As with most things, however, time is a great healer and I'm sure we've forgiven and forgotten. I know I have.

With so little cricket to write about or to talk about, the press and radio boys found themselves the hobby-horse of our slow over-rate and rode it hard all season. We were castigated for only managing twelve overs an hour in the first session of the Oval Test when everyone knew this was an unfairly artificial figure since plenty of time was lost as advertising signs had to be moved to accommodate the batsmen, play was repeatedly stopped because of crowd movement behind the bowlers' arm and Boycott had to receive attention after being struck.

When they used statistics such as that to emphasize their point, I questioned their motives. Yet I would accept that much of the concern was genuine and I do feel that we must concern ourselves with the entertainment of the public.

However, the way our attack was comprised it was impossible to maintain much over thirteen or fourteen overs an hour and there is no way we could ever be accused of time-wasting as a deliberate tactic. It has always been my policy to attack and my batsmen and fast bowlers have given me the artillery to enact it.

Surely, the over-rate by itself is not the cause for dull cricket or else the crowds would soon stay away from watching our fleet of fast bowlers in action. The majority of spectators, I believe, would much rather watch genuine fast bowlers operating at thirteen overs an hour to attacking fields when strokes get their full value and fielders are positioned for close catches than spinners or nagging medium-pacers wheeling away at eighteen or twenty overs an hour to defensive fields when the cover-drive or on-drive, however perfectly played, finds a fielder in the way.

What I do feel is that we West Indians must start thinking of introducing worthwhile spinners into our attack. I know that may sound strange coming from a captain who has relied on pure pace for so long but there have been many occasions when we could have used a spinner for balance and variety.

Indications are, in fact, that the wheel is turning, for the West Indies Young cricketers did carry four spinners to England on their tour in the summer of 1982 and won the three-match series 2–0. When the Test team reaches that stage, I suppose our knockers will find something else to find fault with!

Not everything about England 1980 was negative, not quite!

The advance of Haynes as an opening batsman in the Conrad Hunte mould and of Marshall as an all-rounder of great potential meant two young cricketers had developed on whom the West Indies could rely for many years to come.

Haynes showed he had it in him to concentrate for long periods with his two centuries in difficult conditions in New Zealand and now his match-winning 62, spread over five hours, in the first Test was followed by 184 in over eight hours at Lord's, the highest score by a West Indian batsman at that august ground. He was only twenty-four years of age at the time and it had been a long time since a young West Indian batsman had shown that sort of application.

Unfortunately, since then, he has gone backwards somewhat and he has become loose in his technique, playing away from the body when he used to be really close. He has been playing in the leagues in England, the Durham League, I believe, where the standard is not exactly first-class and where, in one-day matches, he has been forced to play some unorthodox strokes. He has also been to Australia in low-grade club cricket in Melbourne which can do no good for his cricket either. In both, the pitches would also be dodgy enough to shake any batsman's confidence.

But he is a gutsy player with enough talent to become a really super Test batsman by the time his career is over.

Marshall is even younger, an excellent all-round cricketer with a keen cricketing sense. That tour he bowled and batted well and, if he isn't troubled by injury, he will be a key man in West Indies cricket for many years to come.

They were the two youngest members of the team. There was satisfaction for the one of the oldest as well for, in between all the injuries and all the rain, I had the immense satisfaction of scoring a century in the Old Trafford Test – at home, so to speak, at the ground where I had played hundreds of times and scored thousands of runs for Lancashire.

I think those who know me or have even watched me on the field all these years know I'm a pretty phlegmatic sort of a person to whom one big innings is pretty well much the same as another. But scoring a century at Old Trafford in a test for the West Indies and as skipper at that was something special – and I know it was for the many friends I've made in Manchester, even if they weren't backing the West Indies! When the public address system announced that I'd also gone past my 5,000 runs in Test cricket, that simply put icing on a very delectable cake.

So we left England with the Worrell Trophy still in our safe keeping, ready to defend it in a few months time when England came to us in the West Indies for their first tour in seven years. That, however, was not the next assignment.

Our next destination was Pakistan, arriving there in early

148

November for a series of four Tests. Having been there before and knowing their players from county and World Series Cricket, I knew we would have a tough time, both on and off the field.

Pakistan is like no other cricketing country. Its customs present something of a cultural shock to those unaccustomed to strict Moslem traditions and, although the main cities of Karachi and Lahore provide luxurious accommodation in their international-standard hotels, some of the smaller towns are not that well equipped for visitors used to the material comforts of western life. In addition, food and water can present problems to digestive systems.

For all that, the Pakistan Cricket Board did everything within its power to ensure that we were properly looked after and their President, Nur Khan, should be congratulated on his enthusiasm in that regard. Naturally, he wants to rid Pakistan of an image which it has got, rightly or wrongly, among cricketers over the years as being a place to avoid and we certainly could have no complaints after this tour was over.

Things were quiet compared with, let us say, Sydney or London. I did a lot of reading (ask me the plot of any Robert Ludlum book and I'll be able to tell you!) and played a lot of cards (not very well, mind you) and we had to toast our victory with orange juice in the only Test which produced a result, since the law of the land allows nothing alcoholic.

Yet no one ever became crotchety or bored. If anything, circumstances brought us closer together and did a lot for team spirit.

In fact, the one disappointment was the cricket itself or, to be more correct, the pitches. It appeared as if they were specially prepared to blunt our fast bowlers and they turned from the time the umpire called 'play'. In addition, they were dreadfully slow, severely restricting stroke-making.

The result was that two of the strongest batting teams in the world, filled with exciting players on both sides, could pass 300 only once in the series and produce only two centuries. As a disappointed Majid Khan said after it was over, the pitches destroyed the cricket.

The crowds almost did so as well and their strange behaviour led to a most unfortunate incident in the final Test when Sylvester Clarke tossed a brick into a stand, striking a spectator such a blow that he required a delicate operation to save his life.

For some reason, the crowds in Pakistan seem to enjoy tossing things onto the field during play, mostly oranges and other fruit. But they also have a dangerous practice of throwing stones and other more substantial debris.

In one of the earlier matches, I had taken the team off the field when heavy, flat bricks made of concrete started to rain down from the stands. It may have been fun for the spectators but a blow in the wrong spot could have ended the career of any player on the field. Only when the pelting stopped did I agree to go back out.

The Clarke incident occured at Multan. He had been fielding on the boundary and had been struck several times, not only by oranges but by heavier missiles. In the heat of the moment, he must have snapped, he took up a brick from the outfield and threw it back into the stands from whence it had come. Unfortunately, as those in front of him ducked, an innocent spectator was struck a fearful blow.

For a while, the situation simmered and, I can tell you, it was quite frightening as the injured man was lifted across the field, blood streaming from his head, to be carried to hospital. Fortunately Kallicharran showed a keen sense of timing when he went down on his knees to plead for calm. It worked. The crowd quietened and later myself, manager Jackie Hendricks, Sylvester and a few of the other boys went to the hospital to visit the injured man, who we learned was President of the students' union.

The incident once again highlighted the growing problem of crowd control at international sport. More recently, Kim Hughes carried the Australian team off the field in a Test in Pakistan for similar crowd disturbances while the injury to Terry Alderman in a Test in Perth when he dislocated his shoulder in a clash with a spectator who had come onto the ground could well prove the end of his Test career. Surely, international professional sportsmen should not have to worry about such possibilities as they do their job.

For that Pakistan tour, we were without three of those who had been prominent in the West Indies team for many years – Lawrence Rowe, Andy Roberts and Deryck Murray

– and their omissions from the team caused considerable comment. In Murray's case, it provoked another anti-selectors campaign in Trinidad but I'll come to that later.

I don't believe anyone was too surprised that we had decided to leave out Rowe. Throughout his career, he had been troubled by injury and illness of one sort or another and he had frequently had to drop out of tours. The latest was in England when he injured his shoulder while fielding early on the tour and could play in only three matches. It was all wearing a bit thin by now and we felt that we simply couldn't take the risk again.

I shudder to see such enormous talent go to waste and I'll always remember his 304 against England at Kensington Oval in 1974 as one of the most perfect displays of batting I've ever seen. But, like Frank Hayes my Lancashire team-mate, things just seem to happen to him. I think it reached the stage where Lawrence had it in the back of his mind that if he did get fit, something was going to happen anyhow and so he just went through the motions. Murphy's Law, I think it's called – if you think something is going to happen, it will.

In the case of Roberts, we felt that he needed a rest. He was now past thirty and had done a lot of work. Pakistan was no place for fast bowlers, as Dennis Lillee had found out a year earlier, and we had sufficient reserves in any case. As it turned out, our assessment proved absolutely correct for a refreshed Andy came right back in the Shell Shield to take something like twenty-five wickets and earned his place back in the Test team. Our critics are quick to jump on us for any error they think we have made but I never hear any comments on a decision such as this one concerning Roberts.

The other omission was Murray's. It was certainly not an easy decision to make for Deryck is one of the finest wicket-keepers we have ever had, has given yeoman service to West Indies cricket and has been extremly helpful to me throughout my tenure as captain.

Yet it was clear in England that he was on the way out. He was, after all, thirty-seven years of age and it was hard work keeping to our battery of fast bowlers, day in and day out. He missed catches which he never used to and was not his usual tidy self.

This was not only my assessment. Wisden said he was kept in the side more for 'his knack of making useful runs at number seven than for his wicket-keeping'; while John Figueroa wrote in the West Indies Cricket Annual that Deryck 'was but a shadow of his former self' and that the decision not to play David Murray in his place 'was really inexplicable'.

Still, Trinidadians who were not there decided to make this the issue of a crusade against the selectors, mainly Clyde Walcott and myself, and the pot was simmering when we returned home for the series against England. A campaign, in which certain sections of the press were involved, was mounted to boycott the first Test at the Queen's Park Oval, there were demonstrators carrying placards outside the ground and even when we turned up for practice we were booed.

Yes, a West Indies team getting ready to play a series against England booed – by West Indians. I really thought we had passed that stage but I was clearly wrong. We had made our decision about Deryck, and I knew it was the right decision, while David had firmly established himself as a worthy replacement in Pakistan, both as wicketkeeper and batsman.

I thought Deryck himself could have helped to cool things with a public statement but nothing was forthcoming. This was a great disappointment to me for I had resigned the captaincy on a matter of principle in 1978 when they wanted to drop him from the team, as I thought, unfairly.

Still, I had become immune to the hostility of the Trinidad crowd over the years. I was concerned with the newer players, Haynes, Everton Mattis and David Murray himself, and they were quite visibly upset by the whole business. Some of the other older hands were simply angry.

As it turned out, the crowds were small, whether from the call for boycott or the imminent carnival I'm not sure. The start of the Test was held up after the covers had been sabotaged, and David Murray and I had the satisfaction of sharing an important sixth wicket partnership of 75. When we came back to the pavilion, we were both cheered and a Trinidadian friend of mind said: 'We see how quickly we forgive!' Forgive what?

It was a great relief to have got that Trinidad Test over – and to have won handsomely by an innings and 79 runs. Victory first up in any series is an important psychological boost and we had done particularly well in light of all the negative factors which we had had to endure. Steady batting all the way down after Greenidge and Haynes had added 168 for the first wicket and then excellent bowling by our fast men, all of them, sent us to Guyana one up.

Hopefully, we could now all anticipate a series free of incident. Unfortunately, within the following three weeks, the future not only of this particular tour but of Test cricket in the West Indies as a whole was to be thrown into serious doubt by what was to become known as the Jackman Affair.

Not for the first time, grey skies and steady rain awaited the entourage when we got to Georgetown from Port-of-Spain and it was obvious that the only sport we could possibly play at Bourda for at least a week would be water-polo. The Guyana territorial match was abandoned without a ball bowled and two attempts to stage limited-overs matches as substitutes also came to nothing as the weather refused to relent.

All the while, other storm clouds were gathering which we were unaware of at first but which were to have just as devastating an effect on the Guyana leg of the tour as those which had left the country awash for a week.

When England's long-serving fast bowler and vice-captain Bob Willis developed serious knee problems early in the tour and it was obvious he would be no more than a passenger, the decision was taken to replace him. The man chosen was Robin Jackman, who I knew as a good, honest county bowler for Surrey for many seasons but who was thirty-five and hardly likely to make an impression on West Indian pitches. On that score, I was a bit surprised but I had been surprised at the composition of the team in the first place, it was unbalanced with three off-spinners and short of another specialist batsman and one more bowler with some pace.

It never crossed my mind that Jackman's presence would have caused any problems. I think I may have had some vague recollection about him playing in South Africa but so had several others in the team. When, therefore, I first heard the suggestion at a cocktail party for the teams that he would not be allowed to play by the Guyana government I simply didn't credit it.

Surely if that was the case, I thought, someone would have notified me, as a Guyanese and as West Indies captain. Surely someone on the cricket board would have been told there was a problem. Perhaps it is being naïve, although I don't think so, but I believe that if the matter had been raised with the cricketers and the cricket administrators first I am sure we could have helped sort things out without the embarrassment which ensued.

In the end, of course, Robin Jackman was debarred from Guyana, the England team departed, the second Test was cancelled and an international political and sporting controversy had exploded.

What next? we asked ourselves. Would the series continue or would the other governments act in the same way? As professional cricketers, we were all keenly interested in the outcome although at no stage did anyone in government seek out our opinions. Apparently, they didn't give us any points for intelligence.

Matches were stil scheduled for Barbados, Montserrat, Antigua and Jamaica and the cricket authorities naturally wanted some indication from those governments as to what their attitudes would be. The situation seemed to take them all by surprise for it required a meeting of their representatives, held in Barbados, to arrive at a joint position.

For five days, we waited anxiously as politicians debated the future of the tour and, indeed, the future of Test cricket. It was a tense and uncertain period until, finally, reportedly after much discussion about the Gleneagles Agreement on sporting contact with South Africa, the decision was made to allow the tour to continue.

My own feeling then was that to debar Jackman was carrying the matter a little too far. It was known that he was coming and, in any case, others who had also been to South Africa were in the team. My position on apartheid and sporting contact with South Africa had been stated earlier in this book and I fully appreciate the aims of Third World governments in applying pressure for the white government there to change its policies. Preventing Robin Jackman from playing cricket with an England team, I thought, did not advance that cause greatly.

After the decision by the other governments was announced, it meant that the teams had to start all over again. The first Test seemed something of the distant past and it was difficult to get the momentum going, not only for England but for us as well. At least they had a one-day and a four-day game against Barbados to get the feel again; we had nothing since the Shell Shield was already over.

Just when we were settling back into the routine of a Test series, telling ourselves that, surely, the worst was over, came the staggering news of the death of Ken Barrington on the Sunday of the Barbados Test. What an ill-fated tour this had turned out to be. Previous England visits had had their fair share of crowd troubles, but this was like nothing I had experienced before. I felt almost in a daze that sunny Sunday morning when we lined up in front of the players' pavilion at Kensington and, with a crowd of almost 15,000, stood in silent tribute to an outstanding cricketer turned administrator, a personable character of the game who, less than twenty-four hours previously, was among us as England's assistant manager, seemingly hale and hearty. There were tears in many an eye on the English team and I still wonder how they managed to keep their minds on the cricket.

Yet the show had to go on – and go on it did. The Kensington Test brought us another victory half way through the final day which, with only two Tests remaining, meant we could not be beaten. There was a lot of concern in the England camp over the pitch for that Test and it was definitely the greenest I had seen it and the ball did a bit off it all the way through, particularly on the first two days.

Geoff Boycott, who had made a lot of runs at Kensington in his time, was most perturbed by it and I think went into the match having psyched himself out. Yet it was not a bad pitch by any means. Runs were made on it and yet it gave the bowlers a chance.

I felt in particularly good form at the time and contributed an even 100 in the first innings and 66 in the second to the effort. In fact, we were struggling a bit at 65 for four in the first innings with Richards out for a duck when Larry Gomes, with the aid of a few chances but with plenty of guts and maturity, stayed with me while 154 were added. Some of

155

the pressmen rated my century there one of my best and, to tell the truth, the ball did come sweetly off the middle of the bat most times. In the circumstances, with the ball moving about and with our shaky start, I suppose they were right!

The abiding memory from the match, on the cricket side at least, was not so much the centuries scored – Richards hit a brilliant 182 in our second innings and Gooch a truly fighting 116 in theirs – but the bowling of Holding. Or, to be more precise, two overs of Holding's

One was the very first over of England's first innings on the second day. Michael realised the pitch still had something in it and, more importantly, was fully aware of Boycott's suspicion of it which he had made no effort to hide. So he put everything into it from ball one and bowled as fast as anyone I've seen. Standing at first slip, even I was afraid – so you can imagine how Boycott felt. Jumping around, he made some hasty, uncomfortable stabs at the first five deliveries and then didn't have time to move before the sixth sent his off-stump tumbling back in our direction in the slips. With a packed ground shouting themselves hoarse, it was an unforgettable moment.

Later that day, I called Holding back for a second spell and his first over was of similar pace and hostility, although the ball was not new and not as hard. Botham was the batsman who copped it this time, losing his helmet as he hastily avoided one ball, being dropped behind and then getting out to the fourth ball which he touched to Murray. Bairstow came in but it was too much for him and he was out to the second ball he faced, the last of the over.

I've seen a lot of great fast bowlers in my time and several magnificent spells by them but that Holding over to Boycott was, as they say, something else!

The rest of the series was quiet by comparison with the first half. I don't think either team, but more especially England, could have taken any more tension and the final two Tests ended in draws as the weather and the easy-paced pitches thwarted our efforts to make it a clean sweep.

Even though a full day was lost to rain and the outcome was a disappointment, Antigua's very first Test match was quite an occasion for the people of that island. Vivian

Richards is king there, as he should be, and he held centre-stage for the duration of our stay. First, he was married at a ceremony which was attended by almost everyone who was anyone – it was Antigua's equivalent of the Charles and Diana wedding! Then, with the proper sense of occasion, he celebrated the double event with a fitting century. It was the kind of thing Sobers would have done – or Muhammad Ali. That extra-special feat that separates the great sportsmen from the rest.

England could take very little comfort from the tour which was a really rough one for them. Botham, their champion, did very little with either bat or ball and was the butt of criticism for his captaincy from the large contingent of English pressman.

There is no question that Botham is a tremendous cricketer, his records speak for themselves. Yet, as a batsman, he has to tighten his technique if he is to be successful facing top-class bowling, such as ours, against which the margin for error is minimal. His bowling, on that tour, lost something of its zip which, with his ability to move the ball both ways, had made him such a dangerous opponent. He wasn't as nippy as he had been and was, more or less, just another medium-pacer.

I also think the captaincy took some of the edge off his all-round cricket. He is an individual who does his own thing and is often unpredictable. As a captain, you can't afford to have that attitude and he found himself having to curb his natural inclinations.

England's two pluses were the batting of Gooch and Gower. Gooch, a magnificent striker of the ball, undaunted by any fast bowling, met fire with fire and scored two superb centuries at Kensington and at Sabina. He probably would have got another at Antigua, too, but he gave it away with a careless stroke. Why he wasn't able to command a permanent place in the England team I could not understand and now, of course, he has disqualified himself by playing in South Africa.

Gower, the graceful left-hander, probably has more natural ability than any one else in the England team. You only need to see him stroke the ball with effortless timing to realise that. He has all the strokes, too, but that is not all there is to batting and lapses in concentration produced a lack of consistency. When he develops that, he will become a great player.

15 Captain of Lancashire

The summer of 1981 brought a new assignment and a new challenge for I had been appointed to captain Lancashire the previous winter. I had done the job before, of course, but it was in an acting capacity. Now I was to be skipper out and out and I was eager to try my hand at pulling Lancashire up the table.

As you might have gathered already, I have grown very fond of my adopted county over the years and am as impatient as the Lancastrian fans are to see a resurgence of our cricket. Unfortunately, Lancashire have been in the bottom half of the county table for some time although we manage to maintain a pretty fair record in the one-day competitions.

Let me admit right away that I have no magic solutions. I believe that it will take some time to build the nucleus of a championship-winning team and, although we were one from bottom in the first season I was at the helm and we managed to climb up to 12th in the second, I can see the development of a few pretty good young players.

In the last two seasons, I've been happy that Lancashire has provided England with two new Test players. Graeme Fowler, a really gutsy little left-hander who certainly has the temperament and ability to serve England well in the future, is one. The other is Paul Allott, the tall fast bowler who can only get better with a bit more experience and a bit more aggression in his approach.

What is more, I am sure that Steve O'Shaughnessy is a young cricketer with a rosy Test future ahead of him. While a teenager he went to the West Indies with the England Youth Team as an all-rounder and he has done a good job for us in that category. But I would tip him as a future England No. 3 – he is that good a batsman. He had plenty of time to play the ball and a good technique. I am really looking for big things from him in the coming seasons.

What we have lacked at Lancashire is bowling penetration. We started reasonably well in 1982 but, when Colin Croft and Allott, our two main strike bowlers, broke down we found we just didn't have the artillery necessary to finish off matches which ended in draws. I reckon there were six or seven games we could have won had we been at full strength with our bowling. In the end, our record showed only four victories.

Still, I've had two seasons building the team up and I would keep an eye on Lancashire in 1983 and 1984 if I were the other counties. By then, our younger players will have had the experience behind them to supplement their talent and I will be disappointed if we do not seriously challenge for the championship before my days as captain are over.

One thing is certain. We have an excellent team spirit and our victory in that remarkable match at Southport over Warwickshire in 1982 was evidence of that. I've played in some pretty amazing games in my time but none can match that.

Warwickshire batted first on what was one of the most pleasant pitches I've seen and helped themselves to 523 for four declared on the opening day with a record fourth wicket stand of 470 between Alvin Kallicharran, never one to pass up such opportunities, and Geoff Humpage. Fair enough, we thought, as our turn had to come. We got to 414 for six and, realizing there was still enough time in the match to have a finish with the aid of a few declarations, I closed the innings. As it turned out, we didn't need any declarations. A few early wickets, a little complacency on their part, some excellent bowling by Les McFarlane, whose six for 59 were his best return in his career and the next thing we knew they were all out for the old 'Nelson', 111.

The pitch was still in beautiful condition and we knew we were in with a real chance with 226 to win. In with a chance! We coasted it without loss as Fowler breezed to his second century of the match (both of them, incidentally, with a runner) and David Lloyd got 88.

Now that was the kind of performance to make all Lancastrians proud – and to show just what our players have in them.

Internationally, the next West Indies series was that in Australia in 1981–2 under the same arrangement as existed two seasons earlier – three Tests and the one-day series for the Benson and Hedges World Series Cup, involving Pakistan this time and not England as the third country along with

Australia. It was an itinerary which I was again not happy with, for three Tests can be so inconclusive – but no one consults the players on these matters. However, I'm happy to see that, in future, we will be assigned full series against Australia. Perhaps someone has paid attention after all!

Yet again, there was some adverse comment on our selection since we omitted Kallicharran from the touring squad. It was not an easy decision – dropping someone with such a record never is – but we felt that Kalli looked to be on the way down and had done very little in his previous three series. In short, he didn't back his ability and, while past performance does count heavily, and understandably so, it cannot count indefinitely.

In addition, we felt that we wanted to give a young batsman the opportunity of a tour, the chance to get a feel of international cricket, as it were, and we went for young Gus Logie of Trinidad and Tobago. He is a neat, well-organised little player and a brilliant fielder with a good Shield record and he was included.

Subsequently, Kalli accepted a contract to play in South Africa. That was a personal decision on his part and it is not in my place to comment on that. But I did feel he was being unfair when he said the Board had let him down. After all, West Indies cricket and the opportunities it has presented has helped make us the cricketers we are and to say that he was driven to go to South Africa because he had been dropped from the team was nonsense. If he knew he had the ability, all he needed to do was back it with performance.

Indeed, he returned to England to score heavily in the 1982 county season but, by going to South Africa, he had already turned his back on West Indies cricket by defying the ruling of the Board.

In contrast to the team we had there two seasons earlier, we were without Kalli, Rowe and Deryck Murray, three most experienced players. But, in the interim, Larry Gomes and David Murray had proved most adequate replacements and they were to play big parts on this trip.

Larry batted with the confidence and maturity of the high-class Test batsman he has become and he provided the type of security in the middle order which we needed after Viv Richards couldn't reproduce the magnificent form he had on the 1979–80 tour. Larry is a very calm player, never flustered by anything, with a nice sense of timing and placement. His centuries at Sydney and Adelaide were gems and came at critical periods. In addition, he bowled off-spin very respectably in both Tests and one-day matches.

Murray hardly missed a thing behind the stumps before a fractured finger eliminated him from the tour after the second Test. He supported our fast bowlers with a few really brilliant catches and, for a player who was previously guilty of not taking his cricket seriously enough, the success seemed to sharpen his edge. Then came his injury which left him really frustrated – a pity.

His second-string was Jeffrey Dujon, the Jamaican who had been knocking at the door as a batsman for some time but who was never consistent enough to make the breakthrough. The fact that he had started keeping again for Jamaica won him his place and he proved that he had the makings of a Test batsman with a succession of good-looking 40s and 50s in the Tests and a couple of good innings in the one-dayers.

However, the fact that he was out every time between 40 and 60 revealed a certain immaturity which is not uncommon these days among young West Indian batsmen. They seem too easily satisfied with anything over 50 and lack the appetite for runs that players like the Three Ws, then Sobers, Kanhai, Butcher, Nurse and, more recently, Rowe, Kallicharran and Richards have had. Dujon, like so many of the others, is a good enough player to get regular 40 and 50s – and should, therefore, be good enough to convert them into regular centuries.

We lost a close first Test on a badly prepared pitch at Melbourne by 58 runs. It was the type of pitch we had encountered in Pakistan, sluggish with irregular bounce, altogether not good for cricket with batting never easy. Holding bowled beautifully for us, despite the handicap of a painful cartilage in his right knee, and took eleven wickets in the match. However we really let it slip on the first afternoon when we lost four wickets for 10 replying to Australia's 198. Viv was out for 2 and a duck and Gordon Greenidge didn't play because of a knee injury – so you could say that accounted for the 58 runs' difference.

After a slow pitch and the weather saw to it that the second Test was drawn, we went into the final day of the third Test at Adelaide with the Frank Worrell Trophy slipping out of our grasp. Australia had enjoyed batting on an excellent pitch in their second innings and were 341 for four with a lead of 190. Hughes and Marsh were in but the former was batting with a runner after his toe had been crushed by a Holding yorker in the first innings. In addition, Marsh had been forced to retire hurt in the first innings after being struck on the face and Greg Chappell, due in next, had a broken finger.

I believe the Australians were already celebrating since a draw would have given them the series – but I knew the match wasn't over by any means. My brain worked overtime that night. Who shall I start with? I wondered, not a straightforward choice with four fast bowlers. I decided on Garner, since the pitch was producing some uneven bounce by now, and Holding. I also recalled that Marsh had been caught – at silly mid-off in the Melbourne Test two seasons before so he would have to have one now.

The next day, the Big Bird and Holding bowled beautifully, we held some devilish catches and put ourselves back in a winning position. They say catches win matches and they certainly helped us this day.

The tactic of the silly mid-off to Marsh worked because Haynes held an excellent left-handed catch low to the ground. Then Bacchus, whose reflexes are like a cat's, somehow held on to a firm push from Hughes off Garner a couple of yards from the bat diving to his right at short-leg.

That was it. We were through and I told Bacchus then that we would need 238 to win. When that turned out to be the exact figure, he wanted to know if I had suddenly become an obeah man! I really was never in any doubt that we would get them because the pitch was still basically good and it was virtually a limited overs situation. The absence of Lillee with an injury helped our cause, it is true, but the most decisive part of the innings came when Greenidge and Richards got after Yardley, the off-spinner who might have been the danger man, and hit him out of the attack with some perfect cricket.

By the time I got in, we were well underway and it was just

a matter of choosing the right ball to hit after that. In the end, we won by five wickets and when I got the winning run off the first ball of the eighteenth of the mandatory twenty overs, it was one of the most satisfying moments of my career. We were in danger of losing the series and had fought back like real champions, a performance to make any captain proud.

As we walked off, Holding, Garner and Croft, beaming all over their faces, rushed onto the field, headed in my direction and suddenly hoisted me shoulder high as if I was as light as a bootlace. 'Great, skipper, great,' Holding said – and just about summed up the way I felt.

The press next day was full of speculation that it was my last Test in Australia. They had said the same thing a few times before, I remember, but I have a feeling that this time they may be right! Our next Test series there is in 1984–5 season and, even though they keep telling me that life begins at 40, I wouldn't want to continue on past my time.

I am certainly anxious to retain the Prudential World Cup for the third time and that is to be followed with a tour to India, with a one-day series in Australia early in 1984. That is a pretty hectic schedule and we'll have to see how things go after that with back-to-back series against Australia at home and England in England to follow.

It's not advisable to earmark a specific time in the future for retirement from Test cricket and Australia 1984–5 is some way off. But I certainly don't see myself as a cricketing Methuselah!

For some reason, there are some people who are concerned over who the next West Indies captain will be. I'm fully confident that there are several members of the present team who could handle the post most competently and it is worth noting that Viv Richards has already led the side in Test cricket. Larry Gomes, Gordon Greenidge and Jeff Dujon are all now leading their territorial teams in the Shield so they have that experience behind them as well.

It is certainly not an easy job, particularly in the West Indies where the individual territories are independent on their own and are really nationalistic. Their Test captain has got to be able to take criticism – there is always plenty of that – and has to be strong in his convictions, whether it is in team selection or in decisions taken on the field. In the process, a few people will be hurt but that is only to be expected. As soon as you try to please all the people, you will run into problems because that is impossible.

I have been fortunate through my tenure to have had a good team and players who have responded to the respect that I've shown them by returning that respect.

I've also been fortunate that I have had no problems with selection committees, except, of course, at the time of the trouble over World Series Cricket which was an unusual case. Clyde Walcott has done a marvellous job as selector over the years, usually as chairman. He is a man who knows the game and is always aiming for the right type of balance and the best team, regardless of insular considerations.

Any West Indian captain must realise that he is representing millions of people of different territories, races and religions, bound together by their pride in their cricket. He is even more important on occasions than individual Prime Ministers! It is most important that he understands who he is and who he represents and to believe that he can do the job properly from every aspect.

These are the ideals to which I have attempted to adhere and I trust that I haven't fallen too short of them.

THE SOUTH AFRICAN DILEMMA
It has been obvious for some time that South Africa, smarting under the international sporting embargo placed on it, has been keen to attract teams from overseas to play there. South African cricket has been in the virtual wilderness since 1970 and, as the International Cricket Conference has refused to readmit it until its policies of racial segregation are changed, it has become more and more desperate.

I suppose it's the same theory of the caged animal, doing anything to break loose. What the South Africans have done is to offer sizeable sums to players willing to defy their governments and their cricketing authorities to comprise teams to go there. First, it was an English team, then a Sri Lankan squad.

However, for both cricketing and propaganda reasons, West Indians were always going to be the ones most sought after. If they could assemble a West Indies team, the South Africans would not only provide their cricket with top-class competition but also show off that they could host an entirely black team.

I have been approached more than once with concrete offers to go as an individual and to raise a team to go and the kind of money they have talked has been mind-boggling. However, my position on the matter is clear, I have no intention whatever of going to South Africa under its present system and that is that. I believe I have enough respect for myself as a human being not to allow myself to be degraded by having to be made an 'honorary white' simply for the purpose of playing cricket. I wonder if we told some of those white cricketers who have gone to South Africa that they would have to become 'honorary blacks' when they toured the West Indies whether they would come. No, they would tell us where to get off – and quite rightly so.

At the same time, the temptation placed before young West Indian cricketers who have come from humble origins and who have no guarantee of places in the Test team must be enormous. I accept that. It is a terrible dilemma to be confronted with.

However, I do not believe those who have gone have tried to understand why all nations have taken the attitude to South Africa that they have. These include not only black, Third World nations, but countries like Australia. These players have not tried to understand how they, as black international sportsmen, fit into the scheme of things.

If they had read more and taken more of an interest in what is going on around them apart from cricket, I don't think they would have undertaken the 'rebel' tour which has given the South Africans such a psychological boost and so embarrassed their governments.

Quite apart from that considerations, cricket is now rewarding its professionals well and the situation will get better and better. Is it really worth surrendering a potential Test career for the West Indies to be classified as an 'honorary white' and have your international experience restricted to matches in South Africa?

There are those who bemoan the absence of South Africa in Test cricket because they have missed such outstanding players as Barry Richards, the Pollocks, Eddie Barlow and so on. All, unquestionably, have been cricketers of the highest quality and are fine individuals who have mixed freely with players of all races when they have played in England and Australia. But I seldom hear anyone bemoan the fact that there has not been a single South African cricketer of the same standard from among the eleven million blacks.

There is an argument, put forward in all sincerity, that the best way to shake the apartheid system is by going to South Africa with multi-racial or all black teams and showing them the way of the outside world. However, had it not been for the international boycott drawing the attention of the South Africans to the feelings of the other nations and hurting their sport through isolation, they would not have felt the need to attract Sri Lankans or black West Indians. If the isolation could have been maintained for longer, the entire apartheid system might have broken down, instead of making a few small concessions for sport.

16 The Family Man

When I was a young boy playing back-yard cricket in Georgetown, there was nothing more glamorous and exciting in my perhaps limited imagination than the life of a West Indian Test cricketer. To play cricket to the highest possible level and to travel the world doing it was my idea of heaven.

My view was shared by most of my childhood friends and, if I am to judge by the number of young boys who surround us whenever we leave dressing rooms in Australia, in England and in India, seeking autographs or just simply looking starry-eyed with excitement, also by kids in every part of the cricketing world.

The stereotyped image of an international sportsman, is one of the luxurious lifestyle enjoyed only by the privileged few. 'Oh, what a wonderful life you cricketers must lead,' is the comment which we have all heard over and over. Everyone seems to surmise that we jet around the globe, staying at the best hotels, eating the finest food and generally being treated royally, leading *la dolce vita*.

There are few cricketers who would dispute that we do live well and, when one thinks of the millions of others in this world not half as well off, it would be churlish to complain. Yet it is not all strawberries and cream.

The physical demands of the game, which takes longer than most others to complete, can be enormous, particularly in recent times when so much cricket is being played all over the world. The strain of maintaining peak performance and the tension of appearing in front of vast crowds and television audiences can be exhausting, both mentally and physically.

Nevertheless, it is withstanding such pressure that separates the sporting sheep from the goats. It is part of the job of being a professional and there are not many international sportsmen that I know who have made it to the top without coming under this stress.

Perhaps the most telling of all the hardships of international cricket, as distinct from any other sport, is the constant travelling and the lengthy periods spent on tour away from home and family.

The traumas of living out of a suitcase have been well documented by travelling salesmen and they are probably more exaggerated for cricketers. In this respect, the seasons of World Series Cricket in Australia and the West Indies and the most recent three-way series in Australia, with a preponderance of one-day cricket in different cities and islands, were the most exhausting I have experienced – and it was not only because age was catching up on me!

I must admit, however, that the older you get, the harder it is to be away from wife and family. Personally, I have spent nine Christmases away from home since I first toured with the West Indies thirteen years ago. I have eaten Christmas pudding from hospital beds in Melbourne in 1968 and Adelaide in 1971, have popped crackers in Poona and Calcutta in India, and have toasted the occasion with fellow players in Sydney. Only once, during the first season of World Series Cricket in Melbourne, was I together with my wife and two daughters. Otherwise it was usually a frantic – and many times – unsuccessful attempts to get through to home on the telephone. Christmas is a time of the year which means a lot to most West Indians and being thousands of miles away can be a cause for melancholic home-sickness.

Of course, it is not only at Christmas-time that cricketers tour. On an average, each overseas tour lasts just over three months and I have had eleven over the years _ eight with the West Indies, two with World Series Cricket in Australia, and one with a World team, also in Australia. That works out to approximately three years of my life playing cricket on tour. In addition, when engaged in county cricket in England or in a series in the Caribbean, there are long periods away from home base in either Manchester or Georgetown. Even in the off-season, in England, there are numerous after-dinner speaking engagements which are time-consuming, though I naturally appreciate their importance.

In such circumstances, the wife of an international cricketer needs to be of a most understanding nature. Fortunately, the girl whom I married has been that and more, and I think our marriage has gathered strength from her ready acceptance of the sacrifices which we have both had to make to accommodate my career.

Waveney Benjamin first came into my life towards the end of the summer of 1969. I had gone down to spend a weekend with my cousin in Shepherd's Bush in London and, with a bit of a twinkle in his eye, he told me there was a girl next door who had just come over from Guyana and who he thought I would find very attractive. He wasn't wrong!

We were introduced, we went to a party one evening together, and two years later we were married. Until then, I had been a typical West Indian cricketing bachelor, enjoying all the things in life which virile men in their early twenties do, with not a thought of marriage. How fast things can change!

Waveney was from Berbice and I had not known her until she came to England. During our engagement, she was working as a nurse in Kent and, after we moved into the semi-detached, four-bedroom house in Manchester after our wedding, she transferred into a similar nursing position.

It was in the act of lifting a patient while on duty that she injured her back so badly she had to have a disc removed during an operation in Australia early in 1978. You could say, therefore, that injury has affected us both, although Waveney's ended her career, since she found she could not continue nursing and got a job with a bank near our home instead. Fortunately, I have managed to stick with my cricket!

Waveney was not a cricket fan by any means when we met, even though she is a relation of Basil Butcher, but she has certainly caught on fast. It was not long before she was giving advice about how I should be batting and criticizing some of the less orthodox shots I would play. However, I must admit that she is also quick with praise when I do bat well, and she even admitted that she thought I had struck the ball rather well during the World Cup Final in 1975 when she watched the whole match on television from Manchester where she was expecting our second daughter, Samantha.

Melissa, the first girl, was born two years earlier and Clive Jason Christopher, the son and heir to the Lloyd fortunes, arrived on 6 June 1982. Like any Sportsman I like to think my son might follow in my footsteps but, to tell the truth, I am just happy that we have such beautiful children and I dote equally on all three. My main regret has been that I have missed so much of the most interesting years of their lives – seeing the first time they walked, or hearing the first words they said. When I am away I write quite often and easy access to international telephone calls has meant even closer, if more expensive, contact.

Now that my playing days, certainly at international level, are coming to an end, I am looking forward to being settled in one spot and to enjoying a quiet home life for a change, witnessing the kids grow up, dining out with my wife at a favourite restaurant or just simply sitting down in front of the television and watching a good show, all of which I do regularly on the few occasions I have been at home for any time.

My favourite dishes, you might say, are modest but I do enjoy a good meal, well prepared, in a tasteful restaurant. Unlike some of the cricketers of my time, I am not a trencherman when it comes to consumption nor am I one for experimenting with strange dishes – unlike Waveney. While she tries the frog's legs or the *escargots*, I will be quite satisfied with my shrimp cocktail or tomato soup. Naturally, as West Indians, we do enjoy typical West Indian food, such as rice and stew, yam, pepperpot and so on, and, with the large immigrant community now resident in England, it is easy to obtain them at several markets in Manchester.

In fact, I would describe my attitude to most things as moderate. In music, for instance, a bit of soul, a bit of hard rock and a bit of jazz for me. To say that I appreciate Johnny Mathis probably sums it up completely. In politics, too, I take the middle road and loathe extremism of any kind, although I must say that I am wary of most politicians. So many of them seem to say one thing and really mean something completely opposite.

Nor am I so naïve as to subscribe to the view that sport and politics should not mix. Like every other endeavour in society, cricket will be touched by politics, perhaps more so in the West Indies than anywhere else because of its importance in our society.

There have been a few, but only a few, instances of leading international cricketers becoming involved in the political scene at the end of their playing days. The prime example in the West Indies was Learie Constantine who was active in both his native Trinidad and Tobago, where he served in the Cabinet, and in Britain, where he was elevated to the House of Lords as Lord Constantine.

My own view is that West Indian governments can utilize many more of their cricketers and other international sportsmen in their diplomatic corps. Jamaica has already done so with the appointment of the former Olympic 400 metres champion, Arthur Wint, as High Commissioner to London. The Barbados High Commissioner to London for some time was the former Barbados and West Indies cricketer, C.B. 'Boogles' Williams.

Unfortunately, not many West Indian players of my experience appear to have looked beyond their playing days. Yet, for those who are willing to learn, the life of an international cricketer can be the ideal training ground for a career in the diplomatic service. They travel the world, they are, even while they are playing, ambassadors for their country, they meet different people, they see different cultures and different lifestyles. If they make it a point to observe what is around them and to read about the countries which they visit, it would serve them to advantage.

I am not suggesting in any way that governments should employ someone simply because he has played international cricket and give him a diplomatic posting. Not at all. Just that the experience of international cricket is very valuable and should be fully exploited. I can immediately think of men like Sir Frank Worrell, Sir Gary Sobers, Lance Gibbs and Wes Hall who were such excellent sporting ambassadors in their time for the West Indies and wonder whether their potential talent in the field of diplomacy was not wasted. Sir Frank, of course, died tragically young and some posting may have been in the pipeline for him. With some training, I am sure the others are fully capable of strengthening West Indian representation abroad which has become so widespread in recent times. Trinidad and Tobago has recently appointed Deryck Murray to its diplomatic service, so perhaps the trend has started.

There are other fields in which the knowledge and experience gained by West Indian cricketers can be utilized, fields such as public relations and tourism, now so important in the Caribbean. I believe many of our cricketers, with their background of dealing with people of different countries, could be employed to good advantage in these areas, but, at present, the experience and talent is not being used to good effect. After all, not every player wants to be a coach when his playing days are over, and there are several with much to contribute to our societies in the West Indies.

It may be that many of the players themselves are to blame for not looking beyond their playing days. The greatest of sportsmen can be quickly forgotten, as many who have played for the West Indies know only too well, and no one should ever lose sight of the fact. Wisely, Learie Constantine and Frank Worrell studied during their playing days to earn university degrees and, if the present schedule is far too tight to allow that time to the modern player, there is nothing to prevent them pursuing a specialized course with a view to a new career once their playing days are over.

Of course, cricketers are doing financially well out of the game these days and I would hope that they put the money to good use. Many now seek expert advice over investment opportunities, and I get the impression that the majority are far more conscious of the need for a stable future than they ever used to be.

For a variety of reasons, selection has always been one of the most fascinating and controversial aspects of cricket. Those who are appointed to decide on the eleven men to take the field, be it for a club match, a Shield or county game or a Test, have a thankless task. If they choose an individual who does well, they seldom receive any credit since it is assumed they made the right selections. On the other hand, if he fails, no matter what the cause, the selectors are the ones who are criticized.

At Test level, selection is very often a national issue. The public waits almost as anxiously for the names of those who appear on the final list as they do for the match itself. Since everyone seems to be an expert, especially in the West Indies, the composition is discussed, analysed and, more often than not, rejected by those who write in the press or those in the club bars where interest increases in direct proportion to the amount of liquid consumed.

As a selector for the West Indies, I have been lucky that we have had such a settled and successful team. It has been possible to pencil in as many as nine or ten names on occasions with the unanimity of all the selectors. Naturally, there are occasions when 'surprises' are included but, generally speaking, the selection panel comprises former players who have been through it all, who know their game and who have valid reasons for making a change.

A case in point was when we chose the team for the final and deciding Test against Pakistan in Jamaica in 1977. The Sabina Park pitch, more than any other in the West Indies, has always favoured leg-spinners and I argued that David Holford, who has always bowled well on the ground, should be included, especially since he was an all-rounder. Irving Shillingford, the excellent batsman from Dominica who had made his debut in the series and scored a wonderful century in Guyana, had suddenly lost touch as was evident in the fourth Test in Trinidad, and he was dropped. This caused the expected howl in some quarters but the reading of the situation proved correct. Holford took five important wickets in the match and scored 37 in our second innings at a vital stage to help us to victory.

As one who had played against most of the leading players in the past fifteen years or so, and in all the Test countries, I thought I would indulge my imagination a little and try to select a West Indies XI and a World XI from amongst those who I have played with and against at Test level. It should be fun, I told myself, until I actually sat down to the job. The truth is that, with such an array of talent to choose from, it was more difficult deciding who I would leave out than who I would put in.

In the end, these were the squads I settled for:

West Indies (in batting order): Roy Fredericks, Conrad Hunte/Gordon Greenidge, Rohan Kanhai, Vivian Richards, Alvin Kallicharran, Gary Sobers, Jackie Hendriks, Andy Roberts, Wes Hall, Mike Holding and Lance Gibbs.

World Team (in batting order): Sunil Gavaskar, Geoff Boycott, Rohan Kanhai, Vivian Richards, Ian Chappell, Gary Sobers, Alan Knott, Andy Roberts, Wes Hall, Denis Lillee and Lance Gibbs.

The factors that I believe selectors should consider first in opening batsmen are consistency and dependability, and Fredericks and Hunte had both in abundance.

Fredericks gave yeoman service to the West Indies for ten years before he prematurely retired from Test Cricket. He was such a flamboyant player, always ready to take the fight to the bowlers. He possessed amazing reflexes, possibly developed in the early days when he was a champion table-tennis player, and always seemed to be in the right position for his stroke. His reflexes allowed him to adjust so quickly that he seldom got into trouble, even against the fastest bowlers. There is a theory that he was not a master of spin and, perhaps he wasn't, but he learned very quickly and made plenty of runs against the best spinners of the day. The 169 he made against Lillee, Thomson and company in Perth in the second Test of the 1975-6 series was Fredericks at his very best.

I must admit that I did not see a great deal of Conrad Hunte but he impressed me with his attitude to his job, his immense powers of concentration and the ability always to

175

play within his limitations. His record for the West Indies speaks for itself, and he was another who called it a day when there was still much good cricket in him, as he always kept himself trim and fit. He was one who never gave his wicket away, an example which all young opening batsmen would do well to heed.

Gordon Greenidge came strongly into my considerations and certainly loses nothing by comparison with Hunte. Having started his career in England, he is a very fine player of the moving ball and one of the hardest hitters in my experience. He is immensely strong in the shoulders and arms and he uses this strength to club the ball. Early in his career, he appeared to become impatient if he did not feel the ball coming off the middle of the bat and racing to the boundary but he has matured in recent years and has disciplined himself to choose the right ball to hit. I think he learned a lot from his disappointing tour of Australia in 1975–6 and was a better player for his experiences there. Perhaps my one criticism is that he does not more often get really big scores once he is 'in', and that may be a reflection on his concentration. The fact that he is a magnificent fielder, especially in the slips, enhances his value. He is still a young man and his best days could well be ahead of him.

Kanhai was a truly magnificent player, the ideal number 3 with the attitude to the game which that position demands. An individual with enormous natural ability and an almost flawless technique, he was at home against all types of bowling and would be dominated by none. He could come in at the fall of an early wicket with the fast bowlers on and settle in as easily as if walking to the wicket after the openers had given a sound start and the spinners were bowling. Apart from Vivian Richards, there had been no other batsman as exciting to watch in my time, if I say that he should have got many more centuries than he did, it was undoubtedly due to the chances he would take with his aggressive approach.

I have seen him play several dazzling innings in his time but I cannot think of any better than the two following examples. The first was his 108 for Guyana against Barbados at Kensington Oval in 1964. I happened to be the twelfth man and it was a performance I will never forget. It was a key match with a big crowd, and Hall and Griffith were at their peak for Barbados. I think we were something like 13 for three and Griffith knocked back Rohan's stumps early on only to be called no-ball. That seemed to be the signal for Kanhai to cut loose and he just tore those two great fast bowlers apart with every describable shot – and some that were not. The other innings was a century for the World team at Perth in 1971–2 when Lillee was scattering everyone else with his hostility on that lively pitch.

In five years, Vivian Richards has developed into a batsman who fully deserves the often misused title of 'great'. As his captain throughout that time, I have seen him mature from a player of raw, natural talent, who was getting out just when he had settled in, into one with a thirst for big scores. Early on, he was nervous and tense before a big match and perhaps that accounted for the number of times he was dismissed between 20 and 60 but, with experience and the knowledge that everyone had faith in him, he became more certain of himself.

Like Kanhai, he will not be contained by any bowling and is a great one for improvising to counter a particular defensive tactic by the opposition. He has a complete repertoire of strokes and, with a build like a heavyweight boxer, he gives the ball a tremendous whack. Brilliant in the field, capable of bowling off-spin, and enthusiastic at all times, he has become a truly modern Superstar, the answer to any captain's dream. So often he has produced his best for the big occasion, but I believe his finest innings was also his highest – the 291 against England at the Oval in 1976, a flawless exhibition of batsmanship at its best.

The position of the number 5 batsman in my West Indies eleven presented me with most problems and I do not believe I would have been doing any of them an injustice if I had placed the names of Kallicharran, Lawrence Rowe and Seymour Nurse into a hat and drawn for the place. I finally opted for Kallicharran because of his consistency in Test cricket over the years.

Kallicharran is one of the best players of spin bowling I have seen, and one only needs to glance at his scores at the Queen's Park Oval in Trinidad, a traditional spinners' paradise, to be convinced of this. This is not to say that he was inadequate against pace and, at his best, is the complete player. If there is one deficiency it is that he has very rarely advanced to big scores and, in fact, has been dismissed several times in the 80s and 90s. Perhaps his temperament dictates that he does not continue on.

His best efforts in Tests must have been his 124 against India at Bangalore on the 1974–5 tour. Overnight rain left the pitch soft and the Indian spinners were turning the ball a mile. We were 212 for two at the start of the day and were all out for 289. Kalli scored 60 of the 77 runs added while wickets fell at the other end, and he was last out for 124, a truly remarkable innings.

In contrast to Kallicharran, Rowe was a glutton for big scores in the early part of his career and, in two years, had a triple century, a double century and something like two or three single centuries against his name. However, problems with illness and injury affected him, and I believe he became disillusioned because he had to miss so much cricket in his prime. Only rarely has he been at his best since then.

When fit, however, he is one of the finest players we have had, beautifully stylish and an exquisite timer of the ball. I certainly will never forget his triple century against England in 1974 in Barbados and I am sure neither will everyone else who saw it. It was pure perfection.

Nurse's career ended just as mine was beginning at Test level, but I saw enough of him to appreciate what an outstanding player he was. To some, he may be the 'surprise' in my list but he enjoys an enviable record and was a joy to watch, particularly strong and elegant off his legs.

At number 6 is Sobers. This choice really needs no explanation, for it has all been said before. I simply cannot imagine there is anyone who has stepped on to a cricket ground in the past – or will do so in the future – who could be as great as Sobers. He had in abundance everything a cricketer requires – ball sense, quick reflexes, perfect balance and co-ordination, temperament.

He would exasperate bowlers who had beaten him with one particular delivery only to be crashed to the boundary off an identical one next time. Neil Hawke, the Australian opening bowler, once told me of an incident involving Sobers. He had bowled him an inswinger outside off-stump which Sobers shaped to hit through the covers. As it swung in, Sobers somehow realized it was the wrong shot, moved into a completely different position in a flash and smashed it over mid-wicket for six. I have seen similar instances of the Sobers genius myself and was among the privileged who sat spellbound at the Melbourne Cricket Ground during the 1971-2 Rest of the World series in Australia while he played what Sir Donald Bradman rated as the best innings he had ever witnessed – a priceless 254.

As a bowler, he was most dangerous with the new ball, with his late and sharp inswing at lively pace and, if he was not quite so penetrative while bowling spin, he could never be underestimated. As a fielder, some of the catches he has taken close to the bat have been uncanny.

Quite apart from all his other records, Sobers somehow managed to play eighty-six of his ninety-three Tests in succession over a period of eighteen years, not missing one for injury. I shudder to think what he might have done had he trained and practised more frequently than he did, for it is well known that physical exercise and nets were not his favourite pastimes.

My wicketkeeper is Hendricks who is certainly the best the West Indies have produced in my time and, judging from those who should know, the best of all time. This was strange, for Jackie was a bulky man, not at all like the accepted stereotype for wicketkeepers. Yet he was the model of efficiency, not flashy by any means, as able standing back as he was standing up – and I have seen him stand up to bowlers who were more than just medium-pace. The thing with Jackie was that he never seemed to have a bad day with a standard which was always consistently high.

The West Indies has been renowned for the quality of our fast bowlers from the days of Francis, John, Martindale and Constantine and that tradition has never been stronger than it has been in the past twenty years. With our present crop, it is easy to understand the sentiments of an Australian journalist who wrote that 'fast bowlers seem to grow on trees in the Caribbean, as plentiful as mangoes and bananas'.

Sobers's presence provides an additional fast bowler of high quality to add to the three I have chosen – Hall, Holding and Roberts.

Wes was everyone's idea of a fast bowler _ big and strong, with a long run-up and an explosive action propelling the ball at more than ninety miles an hour towards the batsman at the opposite end. In addition, he was a 'character', a player adored wherever he went. I did not see him when he was at his fastest towards the end of the 1950s and the early 1960s but anyone who can crack his own wicketkeeper's jaw (this was Wally Grout while Wes was playing for Queensland) or who can snap a stump in half as he did when he bowled Peter May in a Test in Jamaica is not to be fooled around with. He bowled a dangerous outswinger, had a heart of gold and the stamina of an Olympic marathon champion.

Roberts began as an out-and-out fast bowler, reliant on little else but sheer speed. That was quite enough early on for he was deceptively quick, always hurrying the batsman into his shot. Subsequently, he has become a more all-round bowler, still fast enough but more intent now on control and variation. His stint in county cricket taught him a lot about bowling and about the game in general, and he has developed into a shrewd reader of the game who puts his knowledge into his bowling. His striking rate of wickets per Test is one of the highest among all fast bowlers and his value to me as skipper has been enormous.

Someone described Holding's approach to the wicket as 'poetry in motion' and there is no better sight in cricket than when he glides in so smoothly off his lengthy approach. He is as quick as anyone I have seen, and his fourteen wickets on a dead Oval pitch against England in 1976 was the feat of a truly great fast bowler. Unfortunately, his career has been dogged by injury. Unlike Hall and Roberts he is not powerfully built, and he needed physical training to build up his legs and his shoulders to meet the rigorous demands placed on fast bowlers. Only recently has he appeared to appreciate this and I can only hope that his physical problems are now over because he remains a young man with plenty of cricket still ahead.

Gibbs, of course, was the most successful bowler in Test history, and his 309 wickets were no more than he deserved. There was never a more wholehearted cricketer for the West Indies, nor an off-spinner in anything like his class. His long fingers were so overworked during his long career that the right index developed a sizeable callous. He was by no means a mechanical spinner, instead always thinking about the game, working an opponent out, assessing his strengths and weakness and laying the trap for him. He spun the ball viciously and, if the big off-break was almost his sole stock-in-trade in the early days, he had developed wide variety by the time he stopped playing.

In addition, he had a tigerish attitude to the game, more that of an Australian than a West Indian of his era. He was a perfectionist and set high standards for himself and those who were playing with him. A fierce competitor, he would be giving a total effort no matter if the pitch was flat and docile, no matter if the total was 300 for two and the sun scorching, no matter if his finger had been rubbed raw. I know he viewed his batting with some seriousness but I'm afraid that I can find no position higher that number 11 for him in this particular team!

For the World side, I have made only five changes from the West Indian eleven which may appear to reflect something of an insular bias. Nevertheless, I cannot see it possible to omit Kanhai, Richards, Sobers, Roberts, Hall and Gibbs from any such combinations choosing, as I have done, from players of the last fifteen years.

I have changed the opening pair, and given the assignment to Sunil Gavaskar and Geoff Boycott.

We West Indians know more about Gavaskar than anyone else. It was against us that he started his career in such spectacular fashion in 1971 with over 700 in the series and he returned in 1976 to take two more centuries in four Tests.

Gavaskar is a run-machine. There is no other way to describe it. He does not have the power of Richards, the flair of Kanhai, the elegance of Rowe but he simply keeps on churning out runs series after series, wherever and whomever he plays. He has such strong powers of concentration that, once he sets himself a goal, he seems able to reach it. Naturally allied to that is a sound technique, with the ability to put away the bad balls and keep out the good ones.

I got the impression that, until recent years, he was strangely underestimated with suggestions that he could not play the short-pitched ball and genuine fast bowling. By now, however, he has convinced everyone that he is a great player and Bradman's record of twenty-nine Test centuries is surely in jeopardy. He has kept me in the field many long hours at one time or another, but the innings I believe to be his best was that against England at the Oval during the 1976 series, a double century of the highest class. Thankfully, on that occasion, I was in my living room watching on television – not in the field chasing the ball around.

Boycott is a complex character whose career has been frequently shrouded in strife. Yet, in the middle when he has a bat in his hand, there can be no doubt that he is one of the most difficult batsmen to dislodge. Like Gavaskar, he has no airs and graces about him, just a machine dedicated to occupation of the wicket. It is this commitment to batting and a dread of giving away his wicket that are his biggest strengths for he is not one to dominate bowling, even when he is past 100. Unlike Gavaskar, who has no apparent weakness, Boycott has been averse to left-arm inswing bowling, possibly one flaw in an otherwise perfect method.

I have found only one other batting place for non-West Indians in the team and, understandably, it was a difficult choice deciding on one of so many fine players. Greg Chappell, Majid Khan and Zaheer Abbas are all superb players, delightful to watch when in full flight and often impossible to bowl to. Yet I do not rate any of them quite as highly as I do Ian Chappell.

I have enormous respect for the eldest Chappell as a player and a captain, a position which he would automatically fill. He is a great competitor, not only with a deep appreciation for the tactics of the game but able to motivate those under him. As a batsman he has a fierce determination, heightened by crisis, and an outstanding record in all countries against all bowling. He is, like so many Australians, a strong on-side player but this does not limit his stroke play.

Chappell is one of the most competent players of spin bowling in my experience, but he also took 150-odd against us on the lively Perth pitch in 1975–6 when Roberts and Holding were at their fastest. Like Gavaskar, he seems to have developed a special taste for West Indian bowling over the years and he remains the Australian batsman we always want to dismiss most.

182

The selection of **Alan Knott** as wicketkeeper would have to rank, along with Sobers, as the easiest of all in any mythical World team. He was, pure and simple, the best of his time, nimble on his feet, almost like Plastic Man in his movements and perfect in anticipation so that he always seemed to be in the right place at the right time. He was equally good to pace as he was to spin and it was a joy to see him up to the stumps to Underwood on a turning pitch. Additionally, his unorthodox but highly effective batting pulled England out of a hole many, many times. The closest to Knott as an all-round keeper would be the Pakistani, Wasim Bari, who is built along similar lines and has many of the same qualities.

There have been a lot of outstanding fast bowlers in the past fifteen years but none has quite matched Lillee, who I consider to be the greatest of all. As a batsman, you can never relax against him, even if you are past a century and going well. He has the power to think players out, always willing to try something, never mechanical. Strong and well-built, he has just about the perfect action and, at his peak, was as fast as anyone. I first struck him – or perhaps it should be the other way round – when he played for Australia against the World team in 1971–2, a series in which he made his name, and his eight wickets' spell in our first innings at Perth was some of the quickest bowling I have experienced.

He can bowl just about everything – the out-swinger, the in-swinger, the off-cutter, the leg-cutter, a good bouncer, even a change-ball leg-break. Like Hall, he has the stamina which enables him to bowl for long periods, and his effort is never less than 100 per cent. If, by some time-capsule device, it were possible to have himself and Hall operating at opposite ends while at their peak what a sight that would make, for the spectators if not for the batsmen.

There are several other bowlers, both pace and spin, who had such merit that it is difficult to resist the temptation to include them. Perhaps I should have given myself the latitude of a seventeen-man touring squad instead of a final eleven!

There were no more dangerous fast bowlers, for instance, than Thomson and Charlie Griffith. The former was really fast when at his best with the ability to make the ball fly from an awkward length. But he was not an all-round bowler in the sense that Lillee and Roberts are, since he relied on speed alone and needed the pitches to assist him to be truly effective.

Griffith was a similar type, a really strong man who had the ability to get the ball to lift steeply with the yorker to complement this tactic. Of course, his career was unfortunately plagued by controversy over his action but he was never called once in Tests all over the world and, with Hall, formed a tremendous partnership.

John Snow was certainly a fast bowler of the highest class, one who used his head better than most and who proved himself in England, in Australia and the West Indies. He might not have been quite as fast as Lillee, Hall or Roberts but his bowling lost nothing because of this. Because of his high action, he would hit the pitch hard and he used the seam expertly.

I have retained Gibbs as the solitary specialist spinner because I regard him as the best I have known. However, the Indians, Bedi, Chandrasekhar and Prasanna, were a wonderful combination in their heyday. All of them are different types (Bedi, left-arm orthodox, Chandrasekhar, a unique leg-spinner, and Prasanna, a beautifully controlled off-spinner) and they confused many a batting team in their time. Derek Underwood is another with a wonderful record and if my team was playing a match during a wet English summer I would have to think very carefully about his inclusion, since no one has mastered the art of bowling on a rain-affected pitch better than he has.

However, my assumption in this selection has been that conditions are ideal – a hard, flat pitch with a little help for bowlers of all types with good, even bounce. I have also declined to include any of the South Africans I have played with since they are not engaged in Test cricket. I have no doubt, however, that Barry Richards is one of the finest batsmen of his era and would have scored thousands of runs had he had the opportunity at Test level. Graeme Pollock, with whom I played in World teams, was another South African batsman of great ability although he did appear to be restricted on his legs. After Sobers, Mike Proctor would have to rate as the finest all-rounder in the game during the past decade.

My own position in the two teams named? Manager, of course, able to sit back in the pavilion and relax while they demolished their opponents out in the middle!

First-class record (up to the end of the English season 1982)

Batting

Season	Where played	Matches	Innings	Not out	Runs	Highest score	Average	100s
1964	West Indies	1	1	0	11	11	11.00	0
1965	West Indies	1	2	0	19	17	9.50	0
1966	West Indies	3	5	1	344	194	86.00	2
1966–7	India/Ceylon	9	14	2	760	138	63.33	2
1967	England	1	2	1	27	27*	27.00	0
1968	West Indies	6	11	2	432	118	48.00	2
1968	England	3	5	0	75	37	15.00	0
1968–9	Australia/New Zealand	19	33	2	1292	205*	41.67	2
1969	England	26	36	6	1458	201*	48.60	2
1970	West Indies	4	7	2	334	100*	66.60	1
1970	England	23	37	3	1603	163	47.14	5
1970	Pakistan	1	2	0	45	29	22.50	0
1971	West Indies	9	16	0	545	77	34.06	0
1971	England	22	33	4	1124	217*	38.75	2
1971–2	Australia	6	10	1	370	69	41.11	0

Season	Where played	Matches	Innings	Not out	Runs	Highest score	Average	100s
1972	West Indies	5	8	1	370	133	52.85	2
1972	England	18	26	4	895	181	40.68	3
1973	West Indies	9	15	2	723	178	55.61	3
1973	England	21	33	5	1399	174	49.96	3
1973	Pakistan	2	3	0	123	91	41.00	0
1974	West Indies	9	13	2	621	134	56.45	2
1974	England	20	31	8	1458	178*	63.39	4
1974–5	India, Pakistan and Sri Lanka	15	22	7	1363	242*	90.86	3
1975	West Indies	3	3	0	191	68	63.66	0
1975	England	18	27	4	1423	167*	61.86	6
1975–6	Australia	11	19	1	776	149	43.11	3
1976	West Indies	4	6	0	283	102	47.16	1
1976	England	19	26	4	1363	201*	61.95	3
1977	West Indies	7	12	2	498	157	49.80	2
1977	England	5	3	1	164	95	82.00	0
1978	West Indies	2	2	0	126	86	62.00	0
1978	England	21	36	6	1116	120	37.20	4
1979	England	16	22	4	880	104*	48.88	3
1979–80	Australia	6	9	0	315	121	35.00	1
1980	England	14	15	2	621	116	47.76	4

Season	Where played	Matches	Innings	Not out	Runs	Highest score	Average	100s
1980	Pakistan	8	10	1	275	97	30.55	0
1981	West Indies	7	9	2	728	144	104.00	3
1981	England	18	31	2	1324	145	45.65	1
1981–2	Australia	5	8	1	394	77*	56.28	0
1982	England	21	29	2	1135	100	42.03	1
TOTAL		420	635	85	27191	242*	49.44	73

Highest score: 242* for West Indies v. India, Fifth Test, Bombay, 1974–5.

Bowling

Balls 9829   Maidens 38   Runs 4103   Wickets 114   Average 35.99
Best bowling: 4 for 48 for Lancashire v. Leicestershire, Old Trafford, 1970

Test record (up to the end of the Australia series, 1981–2)

Batting

Season	Opponents	Matches	Innings	Not out	Runs	Highest score	Average	100s
1966–7	India	3	5	1	227	82	56.75	0
1968	England	5	9	2	369	118	52.71	2
1968–9	Australia	4	8	0	315	129	39.37	1
1969	NZ	3	5	0	65	44	13.00	0
1969	England	3	6	0	183	70	30.50	0
1971	India	5	10	0	295	64	29.50	0
1972	NZ	2	3	0	66	43	22.00	0
1973	Australia	3	6	1	297	178	59.40	1
1973	England	3	5	0	318	132	63.60	1
1974	England	5	7	1	147	52	24.50	0
1974–5	India	5	9	1	636	242*	79.50	2
1975	Pakistan	2	3	0	164	83	54.66	0
1975–6	Australia	6	11	1	469	149	46.90	2
1976	India	4	6	0	283	102	47.16	1
1976	England	5	9	0	296	84	32.88	0

continued

1977	Pakistan	5	9	1	336	157	42.00	1
1978	Australia	2	2	0	128	86	64.00	0
1979–80	Australia	2	3	0	201	121	67.00	1
1980	England	4	4	0	169	101	42.25	1
1980–1	Pakistan	4	6	1	106	37	21.20	0
1981	England	4	5	0	383	100	76.60	1
1981–2	Australia	3	6	1	275	77*	55.00	0
TOTAL		86	137	10	5728	242*	45.10	14

Bowling

Balls	Runs	Wickets	Average
1710	621	10	62.10

Best bowling: 2 for 13, v. England at Bridgetown, 1974.

As a Test captain

Series	Opponents	Matches	Won	Lost	Drawn
1974–5	India	5	3	2	0
1975	Pakistan	2	0	0	2
1975–6	Australia	6	1	5	0
1976	India	4	2	1	1
1976	England	5	3	0	2
1977	Pakistan	5	2	1	2
1978	Australia	2	2	0	0
1979–80	Australia	2	2	0	0
1980	England	4	1	0	3
1980–1	Pakistan	4	1	0	3
1981	England	4	2	0	2
1981–2	Australia	3	1	1	1
TOTAL		46	20	10	18

First-class record for Lancashire

Batting

Season	Matches	Innings	Not out	Runs	Highest score	Average	100s
1968	1	1	0	1	1	1.00	0
1969	10	15	1	554	99	39.57	0
1970	18	28	2	1203	163	46.26	3
1971	22	33	4	1124	217*	38.75	2
1972	18	26	4	895	181	40.68	3
1973	6	10	1	271	66*	30.11	0
1974	20	31	8	1458	178*	63.39	4
1975	18	27	4	1423	167*	61.86	6
1976				did not play			
1977	5	3	1	164	95	82.00	0
1978	21	36	6	1116	120	37.20	4
1979	16	22	4	880	104*	48.88	3
1980	2	3	0	134	101	44.66	1
1981	18	31	2	1324	145	45.65	1
1982	20	29	2	1135	100	42.03	1
TOTAL	195	295	39	11682	217*	45.63	3

Highest score: 217*, v. Warwickshire, Manchester, 1971.

Bowling

Balls 4256   Runs 1809   Wickets 55   Average 32.89